Mary's Story

by

Sylvia Zitek

TEACH Services, Inc.
PUBLISHING
www.TEACHServices.com • (800) 367-1844

World rights reserved. This book or any portion thereof may not be copied or reproduced in any form or manner whatever, except as provided by law, without the written permission of the publisher, except by a reviewer who may quote brief passages in a review.

This book was written to provide truthful information in regard to the subject matter covered. The author assumes full responsibility for the accuracy of all facts and quotations as cited in this book. The opinions expressed in this book are the author's personal views and interpretation of the Bible, Spirit of Prophecy, and/or contemporary authors and do not necessarily reflect those of TEACH Services, Inc.

This book is sold with the understanding that the publisher is not engaged in giving spiritual, legal, medical, or other professional advice. If authoritative advice is needed, the reader should seek the counsel of a competent professional.

Copyright © 2013 TEACH Services, Inc.
ISBN-13: 978-1-4796-0016-8 (Paperback)
ISBN-13: 978-1-4796-0017-5 (ePub)
ISBN-13: 978-1-4796-0018-2 (Kindle / Mobi)
Library of Congress Control Number: 2013930219

Published by

www.TEACHServices.com • (800) 367-1844

Dedicated to

John Kendall
who opened my eyes to the possibilities
and introduced Mary to me as a human being

Table of Contents

Introduction ... vii

I ∽ The Engagement ... 9

Chapter 1 ∽ The Matchmaker ... 11
Chapter 2 ∽ The Angel ... 15

II ∽ The Trip ... 19

Chapter 3 ∽ The Robbers ... 21
Chapter 4 ∽ The Centurion ... 24
Chapter 5 ∽ A Son of The God ... 29

III ∽ Elizabeth's House ... 33

Chapter 6 ∽ Arrival ... 35
Chapter 7 ∽ Return to Nazareth ... 40

IV ∽ Bethlehem ... 45

Chapter 8 ∽ Married ... 47
Chapter 9 ∽ To Be Taxed ... 49
Chapter 10 ∽ The Stable ... 52
Chapter 11 ∽ The Shepherds ... 56
Chapter 12 ∽ Dedication ... 60
Chapter 13 ∽ The Magi ... 64

V ∽ Egypt ... 73

Chapter 14 ∽ Flight in the Night ... 75

Chapter 15 ∽ The Slaughter of the Innocents	80
Chapter 16 ∽ Going Home Again	84

VI ∽ Nazareth   89

Chapter 17 ∽ North to Nazareth	91
Chapter 18 ∽ Passover Time	98

VII ∽ His Father's Business   105

Chapter 19 ∽ Baptism	107
Chapter 20 ∽ The Wedding	11
Chapter 21 ∽ Born Again	114
Chapter 22 ∽ Another Passover	18
Chapter 23 ∽ The Nazareth "Reception"	122
Chapter 24 ∽ Panthera	127
Chapter 25 ∽ A Head on a Silver Platter	131

VIII ∽ A Week of Ups and Downs   137

Chapter 26 ∽ The Parade	139
Chapter 27 ∽ The Long Night	145
Chapter 29 ∽ Golgotha	157

IX ∽ Afterwards   163

Chapter 30 ∽ Passover Sabbath	165
Chapter 31 ∽ The Empty Tomb	169
Chapter 32 ∽ The Last Forty Days	175

Introduction

The Bible gives us few clues about Mary's feelings and thoughts, but there are several passages that say, "Mary pondered all these things."

Were I Mary, I would do more than ponder. How did her relatives, other than Elizabeth and Zacharias, whom we know about, react to the idea of her having a baby that didn't belong to her husband? Why couldn't Mary stay at home to have her baby while Joseph went to Bethlehem alone? Why did she have to make a trip of several days to a town packed with men from all over the world who had come to pay taxes? How did she really react to people's snubs and innuendoes and outright accusations of adultery?

Who were her parents? Were they living or dead? How did they, if they were indeed living, react to the news that their daughter had become pregnant before marriage?

The punishment for an adulterous woman was death by stoning. What changes would God have wrought and what other miracles would He have performed to keep His Son safe in Mary's womb and in her family had Joseph decided not to follow God's plan and actually divorced her?

Luke says she pondered things in her heart, but what were her reactions to the song of the angels, the prophecies of Simeon and Anna, the visits of the shepherds and Wise Men? Did it all overwhelm her at times? How did she feel about the responsibility of properly raising the Son of the Highest?

Orthodox Jews still refuse to accept the idea that Christ was their Messiah. They go to great lengths yet today to prove His claims false. One thing they rely on is His illegitimate birth. According to one Orthodox Jewish rabbi, who tries to prove the falsity of Mary's claims, Mary met a soldier on her way to Elizabeth's house named Panthera. This man, he claims, is really the father of Christ. It is so recorded, he says, in the genealogical records in the temple of Jerusalem. Jesus' name, inscribed when he was circumcised, was Jesus ben Panthera, or Jesus ibn Maryum, goes the claim. The inscription of the mother's name was used for those children who were illegitimate. How did that name come to be inscribed in the rolls? Why would they think that Mary had anything to do with a Roman soldier? Why did the Pharisees call Jesus a Samaritan? Was this soldier a Samaritan by birth? And why is Jesus so well-known when there were obviously other illegitimate babies born at the same time?

Mary's Story

All of Jesus' years growing up, He was known as the son of Mary. The Bible records only one time the little town of Nazareth recognized him as Joseph's son. That was when he returned to Nazareth as an adult, entered the temple, and read the scroll of Isaiah. "This day is this scripture fulfilled in your ears," he told them.

When pressed to do miracles in the town of Nazareth, Jesus was hampered by their lack of faith in His identity as the Messiah. And when He pointed out their lack of faith and refused to be called the son of Joseph, pointing out the prophecy that proclaimed him the Son of God, they angrily tried to throw him from a cliff and stone him. How did Mary react to that?

How did Mary feel about the kind of people Jesus associated with when she knew that Jesus' mission was to be the King whose kingdom would never end? Also, how did she react to Mary Magdalene?

The Bible gives us little more than the stark framework of Mary's relationship with Joseph. Tradition says that Joseph was much older than Mary and that Jesus was the only child she had, but the Bible calls Jesus her "firstborn son" and lists at least four brothers and an unnamed number of sisters. There is no proof that Joseph and Mary were not close in age.

How did a teenage girl accept the responsibility of raising the Son of God? How did Joseph come to his decision to accept Mary and this illegitimate child into his family? How did Joseph react before the angel told him the baby was the Son of God? Was Mary aware that the baby would be conceived before she was married? Would she have been as happy to accept the angel's message had she known the consequences? Were all these unfavorable circumstances part of God's plan to enable Jesus to suffer every temptation known to man? Why did God make it so hard for Mary? Why did she have to put up with this obvious appearance of evil? How did she feel when Jesus rejected her when she went to visit him?

In this volume I have tried to answer some of these questions. Little is known, but human reaction is ever the same. Given the same set of circumstances, how would a young woman react today? Most important of all, is Mary's growth and her acceptance of the plan of salvation intricately tied with a metamorphosis, namely, from her looking at Jesus as her son to her actually seeing him as God's Son, then as God himself?

God bless you as you read the story of Mary. Simeon promised her in prophecy that a sword would pierce her own heart. I believe it was pierced more than the one time when Jesus died on the cross. I believe it pierced her heart every time someone jeered at Jesus, every time she was condemned as an adulteress. Yet God sustained her.

Christians today are so careful to avoid the appearance of evil. Who would have carried the Christ to birth if Mary had refused "the appearance of evil"? Mary's legacy is her faith in God in spite of the seemingly insurmountable things stacked against her, her supreme willingness to do the will of God no matter what it cost or how it appeared to others.

I

The Engagement

Chapter 1

The Matchmaker

"Young Joseph has indicated his willingness to take you for his wife," the matchmaker's[1] insinuating voice broke into Mary's reverie. She hadn't listened to the matchmaker and her mother, Anna, until that moment.[2] She had been thinking about a young carpenter who had come to fix the broken leg of a table for her mother. The matchmaker's words shook her.

"He what?" She asked. "Joseph who?" It wasn't that she didn't know Joseph, but there were plenty of young men with that name, and she wanted to be sure as to his identity. She wanted to be certain, more than anything, that they were speaking of the young man she had been thinking of.

"The carpenter, Mary." Anna wondered when her daughter had given herself over to daydreams. "The young carpenter, Joseph Alpheus,[3] has made known his wishes to make you his wife. You have my consent. Your father will be pleased. What do you say?"

"Joseph, the carpenter?" Mary seemed particularly dense, Anna thought. But Mary simply wanted proof that her fondest wish had come true.

"Isn't that what we just spoke of?" said Anna, looking at the matchmaker for assistance. "Isn't that the young man we have been talking about this last hour and more? Are you not in this house with us? Or are you somewhere else?" Mary's eyes strayed to the window again, looking for the handsome young man of her dreams. "Mary!" Exasperation tinged her mother's

---

[1] Jewish custom dictated a matchmaker. This was usually a woman of high character who arranged the mutual benefits between the families of the bride and groom.

[2] The Bible doesn't give Mary's mother a name, but some traditions hold that her name was Anna.

[3] The Bible lists two genealogies for Joseph (Matt. 1; Luke 3), with some differences. Some scholars and commentators think the two genealogies show a stepfather versus a biological father line, or that Matthew skipped some of Joseph's ancestors. Others think the line listed in Luke is really Mary's genealogy; this is the thinking I have used. There is nothing that reveals Joseph's last name. But two of Jesus' disciples are listed as James and Judas the sons of Alpheus (Matt. 10:3; Mark 3:18; Luke 6:15; Acts 1:13). The names of Jesus' brothers are listed as James, Jude, Simon, and Joses, which may indicate that two of Jesus' brothers in that list are synonymous with the two sons of Alpheus. However, since those are very common first names, they may not necessarily be the same. Yet the argument holds that Mary the mother of James the Less was one of those at the tomb of Christ when He was resurrected (Matt. 27:56; Mark 5:37, 9:2, 14:33; Luke 8:51). Mary, the mother of Joses is also listed. (Matt. 27:56; Mark 15:40, 47). This lends credence to the reasoning that James and Judas Alpheus were actually the sons of Mary and Joseph and, therefore, that Joseph's last name was Alpheus.

voice. "Joseph the carpenter has asked to marry you. What do you say?"

"Yes," Mary whispered. She whirled from the window, hugging her mother and then the startled matchmaker. "Yes. Yes. Yes." Her voice grew louder with each syllable.

With careful dignity the matchmaker untangled herself from the exuberant young girl. "I will let him know," she said. "You may expect him for the evening meal." She then let herself out of the house.

Something was needed to teach that young woman her place. Good matchmakers didn't grow on grape vines or olive trees, the matchmaker thought. A matchmaker's work was serious business. She was responsible not only for knowing the character and personality of each person she tried to match but also for making the best settlements with the groom and bride's families. She had a reputation to uphold. She came from one of the best families in town. Her own brother was the priest in the temple.

She felt she had done her best for Joseph. He would have a young woman who loved him. But he would have a young woman who needed to learn dignity and her place in the community. But Mary was far from learning dignity. "What will we serve for the evening meal, Mother?" she asked, nearly bouncing with eagerness. "It must be something special."

"Indeed, it must," her mother agreed.

Mary felt she might burst before it was finally time to eat. Although she helped her mother prepare the meal, she could hardly keep her feet on the ground. She had seen Joseph often. She knew the other young women in the village thought well of the handsome young carpenter. Any one of them would welcome the role as his wife, but it was her, Mary, whom he had chosen.

Mary could hardly wait until the evening meal, but when Joseph finally came to the house, she met him with an uncharacteristic shyness. She watched him from under her eyelids as she and her mother served her father, Heli, and Joseph their meal. While she and her mother ate apart from the men, Mary watched him, hoping he didn't notice. She listened to Joseph and her father talk of bride settlements, agreeing to the terms the matchmaker had already set.

She knew she would have to speak to him before he left, but she wasn't quite sure how to talk to a man whom she had loved from afar and now was hers for the taking. She was still trying to decide what she should say, when Joseph stopped speaking with her father and looked at her directly. "Would you step outside with me, Mary?" he asked.

Her breath caught somewhere in her chest. The time had come, and she wasn't sure how to handle this. Her parents and Joseph were all looking at her expectantly, and she couldn't say a word.

"Well, Mary," Heli spoke. "Don't keep us all in suspense. Answer the man." Dumbly Mary nodded. Clumsily she stood to her feet. Oh, what Joseph must think of her. Would he really want to marry her when she couldn't say a word to him?

Joseph arose from his seat, appearing calm and in control. Did he feel as she did? Did he

The Matchmaker

love her, or did he just decide he wanted a wife and she would do? Suddenly Mary felt very frightened. She wanted a husband who would love her the way her ancestor Jacob had loved Rachel. She wanted a man willing to work fourteen years, if he must, to have her for his own. She wanted to be loved above all other women in her man's life.

Joseph reached out a calm hand to her, and she put her hand in his, shaking and a little cold. He smiled at her. He said something to her father, but her heart was pounding in her ears and she didn't hear what he said. Then he was leading her out the door and into the dark of the night. There in the darkness, Joseph put his arms around Mary for the first time. He held her close in an embrace.

"It won't be so bad being married to me, will it, little Mary?" His words rumbled under her ear.

She pulled her head away. "I never thought it would be bad married to you," she replied. "It's just …" She paused, unable to put her feelings into words. She turned her face away from him.

But Joseph seemed to understand. His hand slipped under her chin and brought her face around to his. Thin moonlight let her see his face but not his expression. His voice was tender, gentle. "Of all the girls in the village," he said, "you are the one who most attracted me. You are full of life, yet you take your faith seriously. You are happy in your work, yet you take time to enjoy the beauty around you. You seem not to know your own worth." Joseph paused, and Mary wondered if he would yet regret his decision.

"There is no one else in Nazareth or in any other village I have visited," continued Joseph, "whom I would rather spend the rest of my life—living, loving, having a family—with" His voice was quiet.

Joy plowed though Mary's being. Joseph was saying he loved her. Joseph was saying he loved *her*. Not Sarah or Tamara or any of the other girls she knew. Joseph wanted her. Really wanted her. Her heart began to sing. Her joy broke out in laughter. Her arms responded to Joseph's embrace.

"Oh, yes, Joseph," she answered, "It will be easy to marry you. It will not be hard to be your wife." Joseph's arms tightened around her. "My time is up," he said. "I must leave you now. I will come again tomorrow evening." Then she knew for sure. Most men didn't come to see the girls they were going to marry every evening. Even though Joseph had not said the exact words, Mary knew she was loved.

Mary was still in a daze the next morning when her mother suggested plans for her wedding, such as the dress she would wear, the food they would make. Mary agreed to it all. None of these details mattered to her. What mattered to her was that she would *be* Joseph's wife, not *how* she would become Joseph's wife. The wedding feast would be the finest ever seen, her mother declared.

Anna led her daughter to a sheepskin roll in the corner of her room. "I have saved this for

Mary's Story

a very long time," she said. Mary watched her mother unroll the sheepskin revealing a length of fabric, white lightweight wool interspersed with blue and gold bands. It was fabric fit for a princess. "This will be your wedding garment," her mother told her.

"Oh, Mother! Where did you ever get such wonderful material?" Mary asked.

"I traded with a caravan trader for it years ago," her mother replied. "I have always meant for it to be my daughter's wedding garment."

Days went by in a whirl of activities as they made preparations, gradually worked at sewing the beautiful dress, and began to preserve fruits by drying them. It would be several months before the wedding, but there was so much to do. The feast would last for a week, and there would be many guests to feed.

Then the messenger from God came.

Chapter 2

The Angel

It happened while Mary was praying one day alone in the house. Heli had gone to the fields, taking Anna with him. The harvest would be ready soon. Anna wanted to choose the best for the wedding feast before Heli sold some of it. Mary had stayed home to work on her wedding dress. But first she prayed.

Joseph had been right. He was seldom wrong, she was finding out. She did take her religion seriously. But she preferred the solitude of personal prayer to the synagogue or the temple ceremonies.

Her eyes were closed in prayer when a blinding light flashed in front of them. She almost decided not to open her eyes. Someone was with her. She didn't know who, and she really didn't want to know. But a voice spoke and she had to look.

She had never seen anyone quite like him before. Tall. Taller than Joseph or Heli or any of the men in Nazareth. He was dressed differently, too. He wore a white robe with a golden rope of a girdle around his waist. Light seemed to emanate from his clothes.

Mary gasped, covering her mouth with her hand and shrinking back. "Hello, Mary." His voice was almost musical, different from any she had heard before. "The Lord is with you; you are highly honored. You are blessed above all women."[1]

What kind of person was he, she wondered. She hadn't heard the door open or close. She glanced at it, but it was securely latched. His words bothered her. Why should the Lord bless and honor her above all women? She wasn't anybody special. Nazareth wasn't even a special town. In fact, Nazareth had a pretty bad reputation, she knew. Her eyes grew wider as she contemplated her unusual guest.

He spoke again. "Don't be afraid, Mary, for you have found favor with God. Listen to me. You will conceive in your womb and you will have a son. You will call his name Jesus for he will save his people from their sins. He will be great and shall be called the Son of the Highest; and the Lord God shall give him the throne of his father. He shall reign over the house of Jacob forever; there will be no end to his kingdom."[2]

---

1   Luke 1:25–28
2   Luke 1:30–32

Mary's Story

"How will this happen?" Mary asked. "Joseph and I won't be married for months. I am a virgin."

"The Holy Ghost will come upon you; the power of God will overshadow you. The holy baby who will be born of you will not be called the son of Joseph. He will be called the Son of God."

Mary stared in wonder. How could this happen? How could God take this moment to come to her and tell her she would have this child?

As if reading her thoughts, the messenger spoke again. "Remember your mother's cousin Elizabeth? She will have a baby, too. She has conceived a son in her old age. She is six months into her pregnancy."

"But Elizabeth is barren. She has never had children, and she is old," Mary protested. The messenger nodded. "Still, she will have this child. It will be a son. With God nothing is impossible."[3]

Mary believed him. She didn't know why God had chosen her, but she felt that whatever it was she could do it. She knew as well as anyone the prophecies of the promised Messiah. Here the angel was telling her she would be the mother of that promise. Elation filled her.

"See me before you, the servant of the Lord," she replied. "Whatever God has decreed, I will do it. Let it be as God has said."[4]

"Very good," the messenger agreed. While Mary still watched him, he disappeared out of sight. *Probably going back to God*, she concluded. For a long while she stayed on her knees in prayer.

"Oh, God," she prayed. "If I am to bear this son, you will have to show me how to be his mother. You will have to help me raise him right. You will have to tell me what to do."

When her parents returned, Mary felt a deep reluctance to tell them about the angel. She felt they might not understand that she had been chosen to be the mother of the Promised One. She wanted to save this special news for Joseph, anyway. Perhaps she would share it with him as a wedding gift. Could she give him a better gift than to inform him that the angel had promised their first baby would be the Messiah?

She simply told her parents a messenger had come to tell her that Elizabeth was pregnant, that she was in her sixth month, and that she needed help.

"Someone must go to her immediately," Anna stated. "How can she be pregnant at her age? She will have a hard birth. She will need a family member there." Anna glanced at her husband. "I cannot go. There is still too much to do to get ready for Mary's wedding."

Heli shrugged. "Let Mary go," he said. "That may be the best answer."

"Alone?" Anna shook her head. "She cannot travel that far alone."

---

[3] Luke 1:36, 37
[4] Luke 1:38

The Angel

"Cleophas and Mary, his wife, are going to the hill country.[5] She has reason to visit her relatives there. Mary can travel with them."

"Perhaps that will work out well," Anna replied. "You talk to Cleophas right away." She turned to her daughter. "You will have to tell Joseph." She paused, thinking hard. "You will have to take some things with you for your trip and some small gifts for Elizabeth."

Her husband interrupted. "I will speak to Cleophas, now," he said. "We need to know when he plans to leave, and he needs to know that Mary will travel with them."

Mary laid aside her wedding dress, but her mother folded it neatly and packed it with the things she would take with her. Mary could work on it while she visited with Elizabeth, Anna suggested. If Mary stayed for Elizabeth's laying in, she would be home in time for her own wedding right after Hanukkah. Mary agreed.

As soon as Heli returned with the news that Cleophas and his wife would leave within two days, Anna sent Mary to Joseph's workshop to tell him she would be leaving. Mary invited Joseph to dinner, but in spite of the fact that they were alone in the shop, she said nothing about the first part of the angel's message to her. She felt a keen reluctance to tell anyone that she was to be the mother of the Son of God. She knew they would all think she had lost her mind. Perhaps she would tell Joseph in the dark after they had eaten the evening meal.

But when the time came, there were other things to talk about, so in the end she didn't tell Joseph anything at all. They talked about the trip, the preparations she had made, whether or not she would be safe with Cleophas and his wife. Joseph was a little concerned. Many rebels inhabited the hills and waylaid travelers for their funds to forward their activities. Many of them claimed to be the promised Messiah who would deliver Israel from the oppressive Romans. He had heard there were bandits on the roads, but Mary assured him she would be safe. After all, she had made the trip safely many times. At last Joseph kissed her good night. Hugging her firmly against him, he promised, "I will keep you in my prayers until you return safely to me. Come home soon so you can stay with me always."

And she had happily made that promise knowing that three months could be a long time or no time at all.

---

[5] Some commentators think that Cleophas was Joseph's brother. He was married to one of the Marys who was present at the cross when Jesus died. Cleophas was one of two disciples Jesus met on the way to Emmaus after His resurrection. The same commentators say the other disciple was Cleophas' son. I am more inclined to believe that the Simon listed was one of Jesus' half-brothers, Mary and Joseph's son Simon.

II
The Trip

Chapter 3

The Robbers

They left shortly after daylight. Ninety miles separated Nazareth[1] from Hebron, the bottom of the "hill country." The trip would take about a week, and Cleophas didn't want to waste any traveling hours. They would have to stop and rest during the heat of the day, and he wanted to be well on the way before they had to stop for the night at a fairly safe camping place for travelers.

Heli packed all the things Mary would take with her on the back of her little donkey. Anna pressed messages to her kinfolk on Mary, especially reminders that the family in Nazareth would be praying for Elizabeth. Joseph held Mary close before they left, reminding her that she was in his prayers.

The sun came up swift and warm. They made their way south and east toward the mouth of the Jordan River where it leaves the Sea of Galilee. From there they would follow the Jordan River south. It had been a warm summer, and Mary pulled her garments around her left arm and covered that side of her face to keep from getting sunburned. The dust of the road splashed like dry water over the edges of her sandals as she walked. Her little donkey plodded, head down, raising his own puffs of dust as his feet splashed into the loose dirt. Conversation, which at first had been animated, became sporadic and trickled off to nothing as the three continued their journey of the first day through the heat to the nooning place.

Where a little creek trickled its way toward the lake, they stopped for their noon meal. Mary and Cleophas' wife pulled off their sandals and rinsed their feet in the cool water before opening the packs of food. Mary pulled out raisins, dates, rye cakes, and fresh apricots, along with nuts and a lump of cheese her mother had packed for her meals. The fresh fruit would not last the whole journey, but the dried fruit and rye cakes would. Mary hoped they got to the end of the journey before the rye cakes got stale.

After they ate, Cleophas sat back in the shade of a small tree; his wife joined him, and Mary wandered away to find herself a shady place to rest. They would wait out the hottest hours of the afternoon and then travel on to the evening campsite in the cooler part of the day. Just over a

---

[1] Most Bible commentators agree that Nazareth was the original home of both Mary and Joseph. The hill country lay south/southwest of Jerusalem. Sixty-eight miles separated Nazareth from Jerusalem; another 19 miles separated Jerusalem from Hebron.

Mary's Story

rise, Mary found the place she sought. A clump of bushes made shade for her and her donkey. She tethered the animal, took a small blanket from the pack and laid it on the ground before laying herself down for a rest. She warned herself not to sleep; Cleophas wouldn't want to waste time once things had cooled down a bit.

But the warning did no good. She had walked a good many miles already, and the heat of the noonday sun lulled her into a soporific doze. She wasn't sure what waked her, but she knew it was later in the day than it should be. She wondered if Cleophas and Mary had slept as long as she had and quickly picked up her blanket and untied the donkey. Nearly at the top of the rise, she stopped. She heard voices, and none of them sounded like Cleophas or Mary. Men were talking, arguing. Mary dropped the donkey's lead, ground-tying him before edging her way to the top.

The sight that met her eyes would stay with her for the rest of her life. Cleophas lay to one side of the creek, his legs twisted at a strange angle. Mary, his wife, was held captive by one of the men in the group. The men were going through their things. Some things they threw to the ground and trampled in the dust. The food they loaded onto their own beasts. Cleophas' weapons were added to their own. The clothing they deemed useful was divided among them. It didn't take long for them to take what they wanted, including the woman held hostage. They urged their pack animals ahead of them as they left the way they had come—the opposite way that Mary had chosen to rest.[2]

She knew God had protected her from the certain doom that would befall Mary, and she was thankful for that, but she shuddered as she thought about what might happen to her. She waited until the robbers were completely gone before she made her way over the edge of the rise. She hoped Cleophas was still alive and that he could find help to rescue his wife.

Mary scrambled down the hill, pulling the leading rein of her donkey behind her. Sobs rose in her throat at the thought of the robbers. An acrid taste of fear gripped her at the thought that they might return before she could rescue Cleophas. Fear burned in the back of her throat as she scrambled through the brush, stones, and dirt to his side. At first she thought he might really be dead. But then he let out a deep, hollow moan and turned his head from side to side.

She reached into her pack on the back of the donkey and pulled out a rag, which she wet in the stream. She held the wet rag to Cleophas' face, willing him back to consciousness. Perhaps he could help her get himself loaded on the donkey. Then she could take him to the night camp for help. Sobs shook her as she worked.

"Please, Cleophas," she begged. "Please, be all right."

At last his eyes opened, glazed with pain. They focused on Mary, then he tried wildly to look beyond her. "Mary," he croaked. "Where is Mary? Where is my wife?"

"The robbers took her," Mary told him. "Can you get up on the donkey? We must go for

---

2   Many of the robbers in that part of the country were zealots who stole to support their causes. Others were simply thieves for no good reason.

The Robbers

help. We must get out of here in case they come back." Panic seized her at the thought of the robbers returning. She pulled at Cleophas' arms. "Help me," she ordered. "Help yourself. You've got to get on the donkey."

"I can't," he answered. "My legs are broken. Find something to stiffen them. Find some sticks and bind them to my legs."

Panicked, Mary looked around for straight sticks with which to bind Cleophas' legs. At last she found some. Taking more cloth from her pack, she tied the sticks tightly to his legs while he moaned in pain. Twice as she tied, he fainted, and frightened that he would die, she stopped her work on his legs to wash his face with water from the stream in an effort to bring him to again.

At last Mary had the braces tied to Cleophas' legs. She brought the donkey close to him, thankful it was a patient animal and not very tall. Cleophas wasn't a big man, but he was powerfully built and heavy to lift. Panting and crying, Mary forced him to stand and drape his arms across the donkey's pack. He didn't move for a long time, and Mary feared he had fainted yet again, but at last, with Mary's help, he hoisted himself onto the back of the donkey.

Chapter 4

The Centurion

Exhausted and in tears, Mary led the donkey away from the campsite, leaving things scattered on the ground. Cleophas moaned in pain as the donkey walked. When the man was quiet, Mary knew he had fainted again. Maybe it was better that way, she thought. He couldn't feel the pain if he wasn't awake. The dust of the road settled on her tears, muddying her face. Fear lent wings to her feet, even as it exhausted her. The sun settled near the horizon as she plodded on leading the donkey with its gruesome burden.

It was already dark when Mary entered the campsite. Cooking fires burned around the area. Around one fire, twenty or more Roman soldiers sat eating their supper and sharing ribald stories. Mary looked around at all the people who were camped. Who but the soldiers would go to the hills to find Cleophas' Mary? Perhaps they would know more than the others about healing a man's broken legs, too. They had to be prepared to help one another in battle, didn't they?

Her mind made up, Mary urged the donkey into the circle of light. "Will you help me?" she said. The soldiers stopped talking and eating and for a moment simply stared at the dirty, disheveled Hebrew woman who would stoop to talk to them.[1] "Please help me," Mary pleaded. "Cleophas' legs are broken. Robbers have abducted his wife."

One man, obviously a leader in the group, detached himself from the others. Staccato orders issued from his lips. Two other soldiers jumped to pull Cleophas from the donkey and laid him gently on the ground. Using their knives, they cut Mary's inexpert bindings from his legs.

"He's barely alive," said one.

"Set his legs first," ordered the leader, "then give him some wine to give him strength."

Turning to Mary, the leader introduced himself. "My name is Panthera. Can you describe the robbers?"

Trying her best to remember what she saw, she told the man what she could.

"You will stay with us tonight," he ordered. "Your kinsman cannot move further until he has more strength. Tomorrow at first light, my men will go after the robbers. Some of them will take your kinsman home, and you may return with them." Mary shook her head. "I cannot return home. I must get to the hill country. I must help my kinswoman."

---

1   Hebrew women, as a rule, spoke to no man they were not closely related to.

The Centurion

Disgust sharpened the man's features, but he said nothing. Instead he offered Mary a plate of food. It was only after she had taken the first bite that she realized how hungry she was. In spite of her worry over Cleophas and Mary, she was hungry and tired. She would stay with the soldiers that night. Perhaps in the morning, she could find other travelers going to the hill country. Perhaps she could still go to Elizabeth's house.

Comforted by that thought, she finished the food and drank some of the water she found at a nearby stream. There she washed her face, hands and feet. She went back to her donkey, pulled off her sleeping mat, and arranged it away from the fire. The leader of the soldiers came to her. "Not here," he said.

"What?" Mary questioned, somewhat startled.

"Not here. You can't sleep here. Come with me. You will sleep close to me; I do not trust my men not to harm you in the night." It wasn't something Mary had considered. Soldiers far from home sometimes did bother young women, but Mary hadn't had much experience with soldiers.

"How do I know I am safe with you?" she asked.

Panthera gave a grunt. "You don't," he replied. "But I'm your only choice for tonight."

Acquiescing to the truth of his statement, Mary picked up her sleeping mat and followed the soldier to another part of the campsite. A sleeping mat lay on the ground, and he motioned for her to place hers on the opposite side of his from the fire. She knew he was trying to protect her, and she appreciated it. Peace flooded her when she remembered that God was also protecting her. If she was to be the mother of the Messiah, as the angel had said, she would be protected. She laid her mat on the ground where the soldier indicated, lay down on it, pulled the blanket from her pack over her shoulders, and slept.

Shouting awoke Mary the next morning. At first she thought the robbers had come back, but then she remembered she was with the soldiers and Cleophas was hurt. She turned over, opened her eyes, and saw another Roman soldier dashing into camp, shouting as he came. A band of robbers had been spotted. But the soldier had other news. Panthera, the leader of the group who had befriended Mary, was to take a smaller group of men to the hill country in the south. All around them groups of campers were rising, eating, packing their animals, preparing to leave. Noticing a group with women in it, Mary walked over.

"How far are you traveling today," she asked them. "Which direction are you going?"

"We are going north," one woman told her. "We have almost reached our destination."

Disappointed, Mary turned away. There would be no company for Mary in their group. There seemed to be no other women in the camp, and Mary hesitated to approach the other men. The soldier had protected her from his men during the night. He was being sent to the hill country. Perhaps she could trust him to take her safely to Elizabeth's house. She certainly didn't want to go home or go with the soldiers who were planning to take Cleophas home.

The soldiers were moving fast, getting ready to go after the robbers who had been spotted. Two

Mary's Story

men were delegated to take the ailing Cleophas back home. There seemed to be no other choice. Mary would travel with the Roman soldier named Panthera.[2]

Once the decision was made and Mary talked to Panthera, they wasted scant time preparing for the journey. Panthera had already eaten. Mary made a hurried breakfast of some dried fruit and nuts and once again went to the nearby stream for some water. She quickly repacked her donkey and prepared to walk.

Panthera saddled his big, white stallion. He rode over to Mary. "Climb on your beast, little girl," he said. "We have a long way to go."

"You are asking me to ride the animal?" Mary asked. "I don't ride. This donkey is just a pack animal."

"Is that so?" Panthera's voice seemed to boom out. "Hand me the reins, then."

Mary did so. "You can't go with me if you can't ride." Panthera held his arm down to her, then. She gazed at it a moment, then up at him. "Grab my arm," he ordered. When she did as he asked, he hoisted her up behind him on the horse. Mary automatically straddled the horse, thankful her skirts were long enough and full enough to cover most of her legs. "Hold on to my waist," the soldier ordered. He handed Mary the donkey's lead. "And don't let go of that," he said. With that he kicked the horse's side and rode out of the camp, his few soldiers following.

Mary was amazed how much more ground they could cover on the back of a horse. They passed three camps before noon. They paused long enough to eat a cold meal and passed three more camps before they stopped for the night. She felt sore from riding all day, and she was used to stopping for a noon rest; but instead of taking a week to get to Elizabeth's house, she would be there the next morning.

Other than reminding her that she should hold on tightly to him and the donkey's reins, Panthera said little else to Mary as they traveled. He spent most of his time controlling his horse and navigating the way. But when they stopped for the night and after he had built a fire separate from rest of the men, he seemed more inclined to talk.

Mary had whiled away the hours on the horse watching the scenery go by much faster than it would have otherwise. Then she composed a song about the angel's promise. "My soul magnifies the Lord, and my spirit has rejoiced in God my Savior," she sang softly. "For he has seen the low estate of his handmaiden; for behold, from now on, all generations will call me blessed."[3]

Mary embraced and cherished that thought, even as she traveled with the soldier she barely knew. God would protect her. Hadn't He already protected her from the robbers and from the other soldiers? He would not let anything happen to the prospective mother of His own Son. She recalled

---

[2] Jewish leaders do not accept Jesus as Messiah for a number of reasons, but one reason cited by one Jewish rabbi was that Jesus was the illegitimate son of a Roman soldier named Panthera. He says that the genealogical records in the temple in Jerusalem indicate this. A scenario such as this one (Mary receiving aid from Panthera) may have led to the false conclusion that Jesus had a biological father by the name of Panthera.

[3] Mary's Song, also call The Magnificate, is found in Luke 1:46-55

some words in King David's psalms and wove them into her own song.

"For He that is mighty had done to me great things; and holy is His name.[4]

And His mercy is on them that fear Him from generation to generation.[5]

He has showed strength with His arm;

He has scattered the proud in the imagination of their hearts.

He has put down the mighty from their seats, and exalted them of low degree."

Mary thought about that for a minute. She still didn't understand why God would choose to send an angel to her. She didn't understand why God would choose her to be the mother of the Messiah of the Israelite nation, but she had no doubt that He had indeed chosen her. She continued her song.

"He has filled the hungry with good things.[6]

And the rich He has sent away empty.

He has helped His servant Israel, in remembrance of His mercy;

As He spake to our fathers, to Abraham, and to his seed for ever."

Mary finished her song with a shout of triumph, remembering the promise God made to Abraham when He had stopped the father of the Jews from taking the life of his own son, Isaac. God had promised then that He would send His own Son.

"What were you singing as we rode?" Panthera asked Mary as they settled for their evening meal. "I heard you singing that from now on all generations shall call you blessed. Why would you sing that?"

Mary blushed. "I was making up a song. We do, you know, when something special happens to us."

"You lost your friends and are having to travel with a Roman soldier. That is special?"

"Oh, no!" Mary exclaimed. Then she reddened again. "Not that I'm not grateful that you are taking me to Elizabeth," she countered. "But that isn't the special part," she stopped, in some confusion.

"Do go on," Panthera's voice was low, inviting confidence. The lowering night and the circle of firelight seemed to close them in from the rest of the world and even from the soldiers who weren't camped very far away. For some reason, Mary felt safe with this man, both the night before with all his soldiers around and this night when the two shared the meal and the fire. She also felt this man would understand when she told him about the angel's message.

---

[4] Mary's song, often called the Magnificat, is found in Luke 1:46–55.
[5] cf Ps. 71:19, 111:9, 13, 103:17.
[6] Psalm 107:9

Mary's Story

"An angel came to me before I left home," she told him. "He told me that I would have a baby."

"That's not unusual," Panthera said dryly. "Most women have babies."

"But this baby will be special. It is a gift from my God."

Panthera had learned the Greek myths. The idea of a woman carrying a child of the gods wasn't unusual to him. Greek religion was rife with stories of mortal women becoming mothers of the children of the gods. He had never doubted that those stories are at least partly true. Yet he hadn't believed that those things happened anymore. Sitting there listening to this young woman tell him what she has been promised put him in the greatest awe.

Nothing else Mary could have told him would have made him more careful of her welfare. If this woman was a consort of the gods, it behooved him to take very good care of her indeed.

To be sure of her story, Panthera asked Mary some pointed questions. She described the angel to him. The way the angel had come while she was praying, the message the angel gave her. She shared how the angel had told her that Elizabeth, far past childbearing age, was also going to have a son. Because of Elizabeth's advanced age, her parents had felt that Mary needed to go and be with her.

"And how do your parents feel about your baby?" Panthera asked.

Again Mary blushed. "They don't know," she answered quietly.

"Is there a man in your life?"

"Oh, yes," Mary answered eagerly. "Joseph. He is a carpenter. He has asked me to marry him."

"And does he know about the angel?" Panthera asked.

"No. I have not told him either," Mary confessed.

"Why not?"

"I'm going to surprise him with the angel's message after our marriage."

Panthera knew a little about Jews, having been a soldier in Palestine since his teen years. Jewish girls who found themselves pregnant out of wedlock would marry anyone who would take them or be condemned to death by stoning. Jews didn't allow that kind of behavior to go unpunished. Often he wished to stop the crime of murder of young women, but his superiors enforced a policy of staying out of the religious practices of those they ruled. And if a religion required the stoning of a young woman with an illegitimate child, it was one less mouth to feed. Herod wasn't above slaughtering hundreds of people at a time. There was no problem with the killing of a Jewish woman once in a while.

"So you are not carrying the child now?" he asked her.

"Oh, no, not yet," Mary replied airily. "I'm not married yet."

"We need to rest," Panthera said gruffly. "We still have quite a ride before we reach your kinsman's home in the hill country tomorrow."

Mary agreed, but long after she had lain down on her mat, covered herself with the wool blanket she carried, and slept, Panthera stared into the flames of the fire.

Chapter 5

A Son of The God

In the cool of the morning, Mary washed her face and hands in the tumbling water of the nearby spring. She used her comb and under her head covering pulled back her hair. She had sunburned some in spite of the covering she had tried to keep pulled over her face. She had to hang on to Panthera and the donkey's reins and still try to keep her head covered. And she was riding on a horse that moved faster than anything she had been on before.

Panthera's garb was more suited to horsemanship than her own, she decided. His short skirts allowed for his logs to cross the beast, and his helmet protected his head from the heat more than Mary's clothing had done for her the day before. She was glad they would reach Elizabeth's home that day.

Without being told what to do, Mary handed the donkey's reins to Panthera. He reached down, and she gripped his arm to be swung up on the back of his horse. They had traveled some way down the road, and the sun began to feel warm again on Mary's face, when Panthera spoke.

"Are you sure you are not carrying your child?"

Mary stared at him. "God wouldn't do that to me!" Panthera didn't know about the God Mary worshiped, but his pagan gods wouldn't care.

"If you are already with child, what will happen to you if Joseph will not accept your child?"

Mary jerked back. "Hold on to me," Panthera ordered.

She didn't answer for several minutes. What if that were a possibility? Perhaps that was why she had hesitated to tell Joseph. If she *was* an unmarried pregnant girl, the penalty for adultery would be death by stoning. She knew that, and it frightened her.

"The penalty is death by stoning." There was fear in Mary's voice. "But if I am already carrying a baby, it is the Son of the living God, and somehow God will protect me from that death."

"What will you do if Joseph decides not to marry you?"

"Whatever God wants me to do, I suppose," she replied, exuding a self-confidence she didn't feel.

There was a long silence as they continued to ride. At noon they stopped at a camp for lunch. Few travelers were there, and Mary paid little attention to the ones she saw. Her mind was on Joseph, the angel's message, and Panthera's questions. What would she do? How would

Mary's Story

Elizabeth accept her? The nearer they got to Elizabeth's home, the more she thought about it.

Panthera offered her some food, and she took it without hesitation.

A man detached himself from the group some distance away and made his way toward the pair; he was dressed like a synagogue priest. He was curious about the Jewish girl traveling with the Roman soldier. A priest by vocation and a zealot by occupation, he hated any Jew who consorted with the enemy. Sadducees were the worst of the lot. They had Hellenized years before and were making themselves rich by spying on fellow Jews. They were as much Roman as Jew. *Any young girl in the company of a Roman soldier wasn't safe, anyway,* he thought.

He meant to confront the girl, get her away from the soldier, and escort her to her rightful people, but when he got close enough to hear their conversation, he changed his mind. "No matter what you think your God wants you to do," Panthera continued as if they had never stopped talking, "You can't raise a baby alone."

"I know that," Mary replied. "God will work it out." She looked down at her hands, ignoring the soldier's evident concern.

Bile rose in the priest's throat. *What right does a common slut have talking about God in that manner? It is obvious that the girl has more than a passing acquaintance with the soldier,* he thought.

"Mary," Panthera covered her restless hands with one of his own large ones. She looked up at him, giving the priest a full view of her face. "If Joseph refuses to marry you, I will," Panthera said. "I will tell the world the baby is mine."

The priest sucked in a sharp breath. He knew who the girl was. A maiden from Nazareth, Mary, the daughter of Heli. His sister was the matchmaker for Nazareth, and she had introduced him to Joseph the carpenter. He had met Mary, and now here she was, engaged to Joseph and accepting the offer of marriage—from a Roman soldier, no less. He had seen and heard enough! He took another step toward her. She deserved to be stoned, whether she was carrying the soldier's baby or not!

However, prudence stayed his step as he took another look at the man she was with. It would do him no good to tangle with the Roman soldier. He would bide his time. He would denounce her when the time was right. It would be better to denounce her in the synagogue and have her stoned in Nazareth than to accost her when she sat with her lover. He was on his way to Jerusalem and would be there for nearly a year, but he would make sure she understood the evils of adultery.

Totally unaware of the priest's regard, Mary looked at Panthera. "I thank you for the offer," she said. "I appreciate what you mean to do for me, but Joseph *will* marry me. Besides, God will protect His own child."

"This may be the way He means to do it," Panthera suggested.

"Perhaps." Doubt tinged Mary's voice.

"I will be there in Nazareth. When will you return?"

A Son of The God

"Four months."

Still covering her hands, Panthera squeezed them. "I will be there if you need me," he said.

III

Elizabeth's House

Chapter 6

At mid-afternoon Panthera delivered Mary to Elizabeth's door. As he helped her off his horse, he held her hand a bit longer than necessary. "Depend on me if you need me," he said. He dropped the reins of the donkey in her hand, held his gauntleted hand in a salute to her, and rode away in a cloud of dust.

Mary stood for a moment watching him ride away before she turned and took her donkey around to Zacharias' stable. She unloaded her animal, brushed his coat with a handful of straw, and carried her packs with her into the house.

Standing in the open door, Mary called, "Shalom, Elizabeth."

"Mary," Elizabeth called loudly. "Blessed art thou among women, and blessed is the fruit of thy womb. How is it that the mother of my Lord should come to me? As soon as I heard your voice, I knew. The babe in my womb leaped for joy, when you called my name. You are blessed for believing. God will do the things He promised you He will do."[1]

"Thank you, Elizabeth," Mary's heart felt full at this confirmation of her faith in the angel's promise. She repeated the song she had made up on the journey south, not forgetting the verse from the psalmist that she had used in her song.

"You will stay, of course," Elizabeth said, hugging Mary. "It was too good of you to come, even though you are much more blessed than me. To think that a kinswoman of mine is to be the mother of our future King."

"And to think that a kinswoman of mine can be a mother at your advanced age," Mary marveled. "Thank God for all His wonderful mercies."

Zacharias walked in. "Shalom, Zacharias."

Zacharias hugged Mary but said nothing. "How are you? You must be delighted that you are to be a father, after all." Zacharias didn't speak. Mary looked at Elizabeth. "Come, child," Elizabeth took Mary by the hand. "We have much to tell you." She led Mary to a comfortable stool near the kitchen table. "Sit down and listen to our story," she entreated.

---

[1] Elizabeth's greeting to Mary is found in Luke 1:42–45

Mary's Story

Zacharias had been a priest in the temple of Jerusalem for many years. His work in the temple was to burn the incense at the evening sacrifice.[2] "One evening just before I knew I would have my baby, while all the people were gathered for the evening sacrifice, Zacharias went in as before. He was in there only a short time, when an angel appeared to him," Elizabeth continued. "Of course, he was troubled. More than that, he was frightened. But the angel told him not to be afraid."

"That's what the angel told me, too," Mary breathed. "The one who told me my baby was from God."

"Exactly," Elizabeth answered. "The angel told Zacharias that God had heard our prayers. He said I would have a son and that we are to name him John."

"But John isn't a family name," Mary protested.

"I know, but the Lord has already named our baby," Elizabeth said. "He has also promised that we will have joy and gladness, and many will rejoice when our baby is born."

"I know I will," Mary interrupted.

"Thank you," Elizabeth replied. "The angel also gave us special instructions as to how we are to raise John. He said our son will be great in the sight of God and should never drink wine or strong drink. Our baby is to be filled with the Holy Ghost, beginning in my womb. That is why I knew you are the mother of the Messiah. John leaped in my womb at the sound of your voice. The angel promised that John would turn many of the children of Israel back to their God."

Mary marveled at Elizabeth's words. "Not just that," Elizabeth continued. "My son is to go before your son in the spirit and power of Elias. He is to turn the hearts of the fathers to the children and the disobedient to the wisdom of the just to make the people ready for the Lord."

"Of course, Zacharias wanted to know how this was to happen, so he asked the angel some questions. 'How shall I know this,' he asked the angel. 'I am an old man, and my wife is old too.' Then the angel told Zacharias who he was. He said he was Gabriel, the angel who stands in the presence of God. He said God sent him directly to speak to Zacharias and tell him the good news. Then he gave Zacharias a sign that he was who he said he was. He struck Zacharias dumb. He hasn't been able to speak from that day until now. The angel, Gabriel, told Zacharias he would be dumb until the baby is born because he didn't believe him at first."

Fright chased itself across Mary's face. "What if I hadn't believed him?" she whispered. "What would the angel have done to me?"

"But you did," Elizabeth patted Mary's hand, which was clenched on the tabletop. "And Zacharias will be all right. He doesn't need to talk to take the incense into the temple anyway.

"All the people waited for Zacharias to come out. He was in there much longer than usual, having the conversation with the angel. I think they thought he may have been killed or something, but when he came out, he couldn't speak to them. They deduced that he had seen a vision

---

[2] Zacharias' story is in Luke 1:5–23.

Arrival

in the temple. As soon as he was finished with his assigned time, he came home, and he has stayed home since. And so have I," explained Elizabeth, lovingly patting her growing belly.

Mary quickly settled into the life of Elizabeth and Zacharias' household. Helping Elizabeth with the household chores and sewing garments for the baby as well as working on her own wedding dress kept her busy. Mary was assigned the task of carrying the water from the village well. She didn't mind. It gave her a chance to get out of the house. At one point she thought she saw Panthera, but when she looked again, she decided it must be another Roman soldier. In their uniforms they all looked alike.

She had been at Elizabeth's for only a few weeks, when she woke one morning feeling unaccountably ill. As she dressed, she felt more and more nauseous until she could stand it no longer. Rushing from the house, she made it to the back garden before she became ignominiously sick. She stood leaning against the back of the house, retching with dry heaves long after she had emptied her stomach.[3]

Once she had finished, though, she felt fine. She wasn't sick, she told herself. Something she ate hadn't agreed with her. But when she experienced the same thing the following morning, and the morning after, Elizabeth noticed.

Sitting Mary down on a stool by the table, Elizabeth commented: "You are already pregnant. What happened on the road between you and that soldier?"

Mary felt the room begin to spin around her; she gripped the edge of the table for support. "What can you mean?" she asked. Elizabeth's suspicions edged into her conscience. "Do you think I did something with that soldier on the way here? Never! I am engaged to Joseph. I love Joseph. I have never known any man in any intimate way."

Her vehement denial seemed to convince Elizabeth. Besides, Elizabeth's own baby had jumped for joy when Mary came into the house, she remembered. "You said yourself that I was to be the mother of the future King."

"Just what did Gabriel say to you?" Elizabeth questioned. "Consider carefully," she warned. "What were his exact words?"

Mary saw the angel again as he had stood before her. "He said," she whispered, "that I would conceive in my womb. He said I would have a son who will be called the Son of the Highest."

"Not the son of your husband?" Elizabeth questioned.

Mary's eyes grew wide. "No, the Son of the Highest. He is to have the throne of David. And his name is to be Jesus. The angel said he will reign over the house of Jacob forever, and there shall be no end to his kingdom. I asked the angel how I would have the baby, because I did not know any man, and he told me the Holy Ghost would come upon me and the power of God

---

[3] Mary probably didn't know she would be pregnant immediately. She wouldn't have so eagerly accepted the angel's news that she would be the mother of the Messiah had she known she would become pregnant before marriage.

Mary's Story

would create the baby inside me. He said that my baby would be holy and be called the Son of God. And then he told me about your baby. I never knew he expected me to be pregnant before I was married!"

"Joseph may not wish to marry a pregnant girl regardless of the angel declaring that the baby is the Son of God," Elizabeth commented. "What will you do then?"

Mary became alarmed. "I don't know," Mary whispered. "I know God is in this and whatever He decides will happen," she said. Then she told Elizabeth about the soldier and his offer of marriage if Joseph refused.

"That would be a strange way for God to work," Elizabeth mused. "But then this whole thing is strange. That may be what you will have to do. You've already shown God you're willing to do whatever He asks. Don't doubt. Just believe. He is leading in this. Just be sure that whatever you do it is God's will."

Mary remembered Elizabeth's words again and again in the following weeks. She knew the only reason she was going to have this baby was because God willed it. She didn't want to do anything that would jeopardize her position with God, or the life of her child. But she wondered how God would work it out. What would happen?

Very early one morning, before daybreak, Zacharias awoke Mary and motioned for her to follow him. She knew. Elizabeth's time had come. The baby was being born. While Mary stayed with Elizabeth, Zacharias went to get the midwives.

Mary watched as the midwives prepared Elizabeth for birth, sitting her up on the special birthing stool. Mary thought about how she was going to go though this same process. She held Elizabeth's hand. It wasn't going to be an easy birth for a woman Elizabeth's age. She wiped sweat from Elizabeth's forehead. When the pains came and Elizabeth gripped Mary's hand, she gripped back. The midwives rubbed Elizabeth's lower back and gave her special herbs to drink to help the birthing process. Even so, it was late in the afternoon before the baby made his lusty appearance.

"Look at all that hair," Mary said as the baby, clean and dry, was handed to his mother. "He will be a hairy man."

Elizabeth smiled. "Get Zacharias," she said.

Mary left the room, sending the proud father in to see his wife and son while she set about finding something to make a very late meal. The midwives left to spread the word, and it wasn't long before a procession of relatives and friends found their way to the house to visit Elizabeth and the baby, to leave little gifts of fruit, baby clothes, nuts, olive oil.

On the eighth day, the priests came to Zacharias' house to circumcise the baby. During the circumcision ritual, the child was always named. At the right place in the ceremony, the priest intoned, "And his name will be Zacharias, after the name of his father."[4]

---
4   Luke 1:59–64

Arrival

"Not so," Elizabeth protested. "He shall be named John."

"There is no one in your family named John. You can't name the baby John," the priests urged. "How would your husband feel if the only son you will ever give him is given such a name?"

"Ask him," Elizabeth retorted. "The baby is to be named John!"

So the priests asked Zacharias. "What is the baby's name to be?"

Zacharias signed back that he wanted a tablet, and he wrote on it. "His name is John," he wrote. Then he spoke. "God has named him John. Praise be to God."

Gossip ran rife through the hill country. Everyone told his neighbor what had happened at Zacharias' house. "What kind of child is this?" they wondered, but they didn't wonder if he was under God's protection.

Later, as he grew, people's affinity for John grew, but he stayed away from most of the towns, and especially Jerusalem. He played by himself in the desert, in tune with nature and with God. God taught him in a special way the work He would have him do.

Chapter 7

Return to Nazareth

The idyll was over. John was born, circumcised, named. Elizabeth had gotten her strength back, and she had the help of her whole village. Mary had no excuse to stay. Yet she hesitated to take the journey home.

At last Elizabeth called her to her side. "You must go, Mary," she said.

"I know."

"I'm so glad you could be here with us. It means so much to me," Elizabeth comforted her.

"I'm glad, too."

"But you don't look glad."

"I'm worried," Mary confessed. "What will Joseph do?"

"I can't answer that," Elizabeth said, "but if Joseph is the man of God you think he is, he will do what is right. Whatever happens, God's hand is over you. You and your baby will be safe."

"I just don't want life without Joseph," Mary said, her eyes welling up with tears. "God has asked me to do a very hard thing. I didn't know how hard it would be."

Elizabeth clasped the younger woman to her bosom. "God will give you the strength," she promised.

"Maybe he won't notice for a while," Mary murmured into Elizabeth's shoulder.

Elizabeth pushed her away. "Don't wait," she counseled. "You must tell Joseph as soon as you return home. It is not right that he doesn't know. If he loves you, he will support you. If he chooses not to love you, he must be given that right. It's not what I would have chosen for you, but God sees things not as people see them." Elizabeth laughed a little. "Remember, God also has the soldier waiting for you."

Mary gave her cousin a watery smile. "But I don't love him," she said simply.

"God will give you love if that is what he has for you." Elizabeth gave her a little shake. "Never doubt God."

Mary straightened. "No. You're right. I will go pack my things."

The trip back to Nazareth was much slower than when Mary had come to Elizabeth's house. No big, fleet horse carried her fifty miles in one day. Her little donkey had grown fat and lazy while she sat in the house helping Elizabeth. He didn't like the idea of carrying a pack again and walking all those miles.

Even though Zacharias and Mary had begun the journey on the first day of the week, it took them more than a week to reach Nazareth. They spent the Sabbath at Salim, leaving at first light the next day to reach home two days later. Zacharias stayed long enough to share his story with Mary's parents.

Joseph came over as soon as Mary came home. His smile as wide as his arms, he embraced Mary. "I will never let you go away again," he warned.

Mary gave him a sad smile. "I hope that is true," she said. Taking her courage hard in both hands, she looked Joseph in the eyes. "There is something I must tell you," she said. She led Joseph into the house where Zacharias and her parents sat. Zacharias reached out and squeezed her hand as she passed by him. She felt grateful for his strength and support. "I must tell you," she repeated. "Zacharias knows and Elizabeth knows, and they believe that God is leading me. I am with child."

An awful silence filled the house.

Mary didn't want to look to Joseph. The horror on her mother's face was enough. Why did God have to make it so hard, she wondered again. Zacharias broke the silence. "You know the story of the child Elizabeth has. It is the forerunner of the Messiah. Mary's baby will be the Messiah."

"So say you." Heli's voice sounded rough and foreign to Mary's ears.

Joseph stood, pushing his stool over as he did so. He started for the door. Mary reached for his hand, but he jerked it away. Without a word he passed out of the door, perhaps out of her life forever. It hurt too much to cry. Mary sat staring at the door.

"What did you expect?" her mother's words cut the wound even deeper. "He trusted you. What happened on that trip to Zacharias' and Elizabeth's? Why didn't you come back with Cleophas? You know they found his wife harmed by those robbers. How could you bring such reproach on your father's house?"

Mary looked at her mother. Fierce anger burned from Anna's eyes. "You may have fooled an old fool like Zacharias, who thinks his son is special because he was born in his father's old age. But you won't fool me. Something happened on that trip. I never believed my daughter would be a harlot. Give me back your wedding dress!"

Mary's heart constricted. "Mother, you don't mean it!"

"I mean it!" Anna strode to Mary's room, where she frantically broke open the pack. Jerking out the garment that Mary and Elizabeth had worked on so many hours, she tore the dress in two. "You will never wear this! You are no longer my daughter!"

The back of Mary's throat burned, but still she didn't cry. The angel hadn't told her what to say to her parents. The angel hadn't told her how to tell Joseph. Why had God asked her to do such a hard thing?

Mary's Story

"Anna, you don't know what you are saying," Zacharias said in an effort to calm her.

"I know," Anna replied, almost spitting the words at him. "You may stay tonight because you are my kinsman. Tomorrow morning you may take that slut with you and leave my house. As long as you support her, you are not welcome here either."

"Heli?" Zacharias looked at Mary's father. But Heli stood and, following Joseph's example, walked out the door. Mary had never felt more alone in all her life.

Joseph walked aimlessly. He thought he knew Mary. He thought she took her religion seriously. He thought she was the kind of good, loyal person who would make a perfect wife. That just showed how little anyone could know another person. What should he do? If he publicly denounced her, the priests would stone her to death. But he couldn't marry her. Not if she carried another man's child.

For hours Joseph walked the darkened streets of Nazareth. He fought the love he had for Mary, and he fought the despair. At last he found himself away from the town, heading down the road to the Sea of Galilee. *He should turn back*, he thought. Zealots were all over, and the roads at night were far from safe. But he kept walking. Life wasn't worth living without Mary; life wasn't worth living with her. An unfaithful woman was the last thing he wanted in his life.

Toward dawn he came to a decision. He would divorce her privately.[1] He would set her up in her own house. He would support her and her child, but he would not live with her. She would never be his wife. The decision made, he felt a great weariness of spirit. Finding a grassy place beside the road and losing sight of his own safety, he lay down and slept for a while.

The sun was just coming up, when someone touched Joseph's shoulder. Jerked awake by the thought of robbers, he sat up quickly. He had never seen an angel before, but he had no doubt who he was.

The angel spoke. "Joseph, thou son of David, don't be afraid to take Mary for your wife. The baby she is carrying is conceived in her of the Holy Ghost. She will have a son. You are to name him Jesus. He shall save his people from their sins."

The angel stood quietly and watched Joseph as if to see whether his words had made the desired impression. Then he disappeared. As if the angel were still talking to him, Joseph remembered the prophecy of the Messiah. "Behold a virgin shall be with child, and shall bring forth a son, and they shall call his name Emmanuel, which being interpreted is, 'God with us.'"

Wide awake now, Joseph jumped to his feet. He started back toward Nazareth. It was true; he hadn't given Mary a chance to explain. He had condemned her without trial. Regret lent wings to his feet as he hurried back to the village. It was still very early when he entered the streets of town. He wanted to go directly to Heli's house and tell Mary he loved her and would marry her.

---
1   Joseph's struggle to accept Mary's child is recorded in Matthew 1:18–25.

Return to Nazareth

But glancing at the clothes he had slept in, he decided he must go home and clean up first.

Joseph found a man waiting beside his door. A Roman soldier. The soldier stood as Joseph walked up to the house. People often asked Joseph to work for them, but there was no reason for someone to expect him to work that early in the morning. Impatience tinged his voice as he asked the man what work he wanted done.

"No work," the soldier replied. "My name is Panthera. I met Mary on the road to Jerusalem. I took her to her kinsman's house. I wish to know what you are going to do. If you will not marry her and raise God's child with her, I will."

In stunned surprise Joseph looked at this Gentile, this man who had no belief in the true God of Israel yet had so much more faith that the child Mary carried was the Son of God. Joseph didn't say anything. "Are you going to take her as your wife?" Panthera pressed.

It wasn't any of the man's business, Joseph thought. But he answered, "I am going to marry her. Today." The soldier nodded. He raised his hand in a salute and walked away.

Mary wasn't fully awake when the rap came at the door. Heli stumbled from his bed to answer. Joseph stood there. "May I come in?"

"Shalom, Joseph. Enter," Heli said, backing away from the door. "We must make some decision this morning."

"The decision is made," Joseph replied. Fear gripped Mary. What decision had Joseph made? Then she remembered Elizabeth's words, "God will protect you and His child."

"Mary," Joseph called. Mary smoothed her nightdress and stepped out of the bedroom. "Put on your wedding dress. Today is your wedding day." A sob broke from Mary's throat as she flew across the room into Joseph's arms.

"Thank God," Zacharias spoke from the doorway of the next room.

"I hope you will not live to regret this day's work," Anna said bitterly. "She has no wedding dress."

IV
Bethlehem

Chapter 8

Married

Mary and Joseph settled into domesticity. Although Joseph was the most attentive husband Mary could have asked for, she had some regrets. Joseph gave her a lovely room. His carpentry skills resulted in some beautiful furnishings for their home, but Joseph refused to really make her his wife.[1]

Sometimes, during the night when Mary couldn't sleep, she wondered if she would ever become Joseph's real wife. Sometimes, frightened, she wondered if this wonderful gift of God's Son as her son would permanently divorce her from Joseph; if she was destined to always be his wife in name only.

One day, catching Joseph at a lull in his work, she approached him. "Joseph," she uttered his name tentatively. He was always kind to her, but she felt his distance.

Joseph turned. His face reflected the uncertainty she felt. "What is it, Mary?"

"Joseph …" Tears filled Mary's eyes. Her voice choked. How could she tell this man, whom she loved so much, how frightened she was? But she didn't need to.

Joseph took two swift steps to her side, folded her in his muscular arms, and held her weeping. Sobs racked her body while Joseph just held her. At last she whispered, "I'm so scared, Joseph."

His arms tightened. "I am too, Mary."

"What is God asking us to do?" Mary hiccupped. "What will this baby be like? How can we be parents to the Messiah?" At each question, Mary's voice grew a little more hysterical.

"Sh-h-h-h." Joseph clumsily patted her back. "God will lead us. He will tell us how to raise this child."

"Do you really think so? Isn't that why God gave us parents—to help us with decisions, to teach us how to teach our children? My mother will not even talk to me. My father turned his back on me yesterday. How are we to learn?"

"God will teach us," Joseph reiterated. He thought of what had happened to him just the day before. He had walked into the synagogue for evening sacrifice, and conversation all around him stopped. Men stopped to stare. Stories were circulating. Everyone knew the baby Mary carried

---
1 Matt. 1:25

was not his. Some men were a little too friendly, a little too jovial. Others stood back to see what might happen to him. Some men ignored him completely. Among those was Heli. It really hurt when some acted as if he were a hero for taking a woman as his wife who, they supposed, hadn't been true to him. Others derided him as less than a man because his wife wasn't satisfied with one husband.

The barbs weren't always open and malicious, but they were there. Joseph felt the strain. More than anything he wanted to take Mary fully to be his wife, but he felt he might somehow pollute that holy thing that was growing inside her. So in spite of the fact that Mary needed his love and strength, he stayed away from her bed at night. He didn't think he could keep himself from loving her if she was by his side.

Now as he felt Mary tremble in his arms, Joseph knew he had somehow let her down. "God will lead us, Mary," he told her. "Both of us. We are in this together, you know. You, me, God, and the baby. I love you, Mary."

Mary wrapped her arms more tightly around Joseph's waist. "I guess I just needed to hear that I'm not alone," she told him. "Sometimes, especially at night, I feel so alone."

"I know," Joseph replied. "Sometimes, especially at night, I feel the same way."

"Can't we be together at night, Joseph?"

"Oh, Mary." Joseph held her against himself. "I don't know."

"Maybe it will be easier now knowing you care," Mary whispered.

"I care," Joseph replied fiercely. "Oh, yes, Mary. I care."

Things seemed a little better after that, especially at home, but Mary felt the eyes of the village on her as she went about her work. Women near the well would stop talking when she walked up. Men were a little more friendly than they should be, friendlier than they were to women without a cloud of suspicion above their heads. There were times she thought she would have to ask Joseph to do her errands for her. And then she thought she couldn't do that to him.

In spite of the fact that Joseph had made her an "honest woman," she sensed the condemnation of those around her, and she especially missed the relationship she had previously enjoyed with her mother. She wondered if her mother would ever come to forgive her and if her father would ever stop turning his back on her. The baby was growing inside her, but Mary lost weight.

Chapter 9

To Be Taxed

They had been married almost five months when Joseph came into the house one evening. "Mary, we are leaving," he said flatly.

"Leaving?" Mary could do nothing but stare at him for a moment. "Where are we going?"

"Two years ago Caesar Augustus ordered a census of the whole Roman empire," Joseph replied. "Now the decision has been made that every man must be counted in the place of his birth."

"Bethlehem? Joseph I can't travel to Bethlehem. It's almost time for the baby to be born."[1]

Anguish clouded Joseph's face. "I can't leave you here," he said. "Who would take care of you? There are no women in the village who will help you. I've seen the way men look at you. You wouldn't be safe with me gone."

Reluctantly Mary acknowledged the truth of his words. "When will we leave?" she asked.

Joseph released the breath he had been holding. "Just as soon as you can be ready," he replied. "I want to take the trip in easy stages so it will not be hard for you, but we must get there in time to find a place to live before the baby is born."

"It shouldn't take long to get ready." Mary looked around the house. She knew she had to take clothes for them and the baby. Food to eat. There were some things Joseph had made that she didn't want to leave behind. She hurried to pack everything she wanted to take with her.

Mary realized the seriousness of Joseph's commitment to leaving when she entered his workshop later that day to tell him she had nearly finished her preparations. The pegs that usually held his tools were empty. A pack for the donkey lay on the floor filled with the things he worked with and some small pieces of wood. After seeing what Joseph was doing, she entered her home with new eyes.

Carefully she went from room to room, making sure she was taking only what she needed. In a special pouch she packed the soft swaddling cloths she had made for the baby. Blankets, sleeping mats and clothes, cooking pots and food, candles, olive oil, and lamps. All those went

---

[1] Only Joseph was required to go to Bethlehem and be counted; the women did not have to go. Although the Bible does not specify the reason Joseph took Mary along on the trip to Bethlehem, there had to be a good reason Mary did not to stay at home with relatives and midwives when she was so close to her due date.

into other packs. She saved out her sleeping mat, one blanket for the night, and enough food for the breakfast meal before they began the journey. Then she lay down to sleep.

She had almost fallen sleep when Joseph entered the room. It was the first time in their married life he had come to her at night. "Do you mind if I sleep with you tonight?" he asked diffidently.

"Why tonight?"

"I packed my sleeping mat on the bottom," he said ruefully.

Mary smiled, edged over on her mat, and opened the blanket. Joseph lay down beside her, covering himself with his side of the blanket.

They lay there, stiffly trying to sleep. Neither of them spoke. At last Joseph turned toward Mary. Gathering her in his arms, he pulled her back against his body. Mary felt the warmth of her husband's arms and relaxed. "Now I feel we are truly married," she murmured.

A chuckle rumbled behind her ear. "Not yet, Mary," her husband replied.

They left at dawn. There was no one to see them off on their journey. Unlike the trip to the hill country nine months before, they began this journey without warm food and without her parents' blessing before departure. Mary felt the difference of the journey, but she knew that Joseph loved her, and she knew she was under God's protection. In spite of all her doubts that she could be the kind of mother the Messiah needed, she knew God would protect her because of the child she carried.

Whenever she was freshly rested, Mary walked. When she tired, Joseph helped her on top of the packs the faithful donkey carried. They stopped early for the midday meal, and Joseph spread her sleeping mat so she could rest before they continued their journey. Mary was thankful for his care, but after several days of it, she suggested that they move a little more quickly. "The baby will be born without a home if we take much longer," she teased him.

It took them ten days, with Joseph's careful watch over rest times, to reach Bethlehem. It being the last day on the road, Joseph, noticing the strain on Mary's face, wanted to stop more often, but she insisted on keeping the pace. I want to reach shelter tonight," she told him.

Confident that they would find a roof over their heads, Joseph plodded on through the spring sunlight. The sun was nearly touching the western horizon when they found their way into town.

Camels and donkeys vied for space in the busy streets of Bethlehem. Caravans carrying wares jostled people on foot. Smells of spices in the caravans mingled with the odor of the animals themselves. The noise of hundreds of people and animals made enough of a din to give Mary a headache. She stared around her, open-mouthed. "The whole world must be here to be counted and taxed," she exclaimed. Joseph looked almost as awed.

"We must find an inn," he replied. They stopped at the first place they found. Mary sat on the donkey while Joseph went to inquire about a room. But he came back shaking his head.

To Be Taxed

"There is no place to put even a mat on the floor there."

They tried three more places, but there was no space to stay wherever they stopped. At the fourth place, Joseph came out of the inn with a more resigned look than ever. "I'm sorry Mary," he said. "I had hoped to have a place you could sleep inside tonight, but it looks like we will have to camp out again."

Exhausted, Mary put her hand on her husband's head.

"You've done your best," she encouraged him. "God is still with us."

Joseph gripped the donkey's lead in his hand and began walking again. There seemed no end to the people they still passed in the streets, though it was nearly fully dark now. He hoped he could find even a place in a camping area where he could feel safe with Mary and her precious burden.

Chapter 10

The Stable

At the edge of town Joseph saw one more inn. "I doubt it will do any good to ask," Mary said.

"Probably not," Joseph agreed. He almost walked past without stopping. Then he glanced again at Mary's face. He had to try. The innkeeper was turning away another traveler when Joseph walked up. There was no chance they would find a bed for the night. "Have you any room at all?" Joseph asked.[1]

The man glanced at him and then at the woman sitting on the donkey, whom he observed to be worn out and obviously pregnant. He couldn't understand why a man would travel with a woman who was so close to her time. But her obvious suffering stopped his thoughts. All I have is a stall in the stable. He said. "It isn't much, but it's clean and it's out of the weather."

"Thank you," Joseph answered, with feeling. "It's better than camping somewhere."

The innkeeper led them around to the back. The stable was good-sized. Horses, donkeys, a few sheep, a couple of goats, travelers' packs, all vied for space. He led them to the back of the stable. The stall, as he said, was fairly clean. He pointed to a couple bales of straw. "You can spread that around for your bed if you like," he said. "I'll make sure you have some hot water and a meal. I need to get back." He left the candle he had carried in a holder on the wall.

Joseph opened one bale of straw and spread it on the floor. He helped Mary off the donkey, and she dropped onto the bale he hadn't opened. It had been a very long day. He lifted the packs from the donkey's back and found Mary's sleeping mat and blanket on top. They hadn't bothered to find Joseph's mat the whole of their trip. Mary secretly smiled to herself as he spread the mat and blanket on the straw.

A servant brought a pot of water and some food. Mary washed, but she was too tired to eat much. Instead, she lay down on the sleeping mat and almost immediately fell into a sound sleep. Joseph sat for a while looking at his wife. He regretted the necessity of bringing her on this long trip, especially now. He loved her so much. He hated the hurts she had suffered at the slights of the townspeople, and especially her parents' attitude toward this girl they had loved so well. He wondered why things had happened as they had.

---

1   Luke 2:1–7

The Stable

At last he blew out the candle, shuffled through the straw, and lay down beside Mary. The barn was warm compared to the nights they had spent in the open. Tired himself, Joseph soon fell asleep.

Sometime after the middle of the night, Mary awoke to a sharp pain. She held her breath as the pain deepened. It felt like something had tightened around her and she could hardly breathe. It took a few moments of waking before she realized what was happening. She couldn't have the baby now, she thought wildly. She didn't even have a birthing stool.

The pain eased. Mary held her breath and waited, but nothing more happened. Perhaps it was because she was tired, she told herself. She settled closer to Joseph and tried to go back to sleep. But sleep eluded her, and in only a few minutes, she felt another pain building. Again she held her breath while the pain built, pushing the insides of her body into a spasm upon which she focused her whole being.

As the pain passed, she stirred restlessly. Immediately Joseph woke up. Mary," he murmured, "is something wrong?"

"I think I am having the baby," Mary gasped as another pain shot through her.

Momentarily Joseph lost his head. He jumped from the sleeping mat, lit the candle, and ran his hands through his hair. "What shall I do?" he asked. "I don't know anything about birthing a baby. I don't know where the midwives are in this town. How long have you been in pain?"

"My back ached all afternoon," Mary confessed. "I thought it was just from riding."

"I don't know anything about birthing a baby," Joseph repeated.

Mary gasped again, reaching for Joseph's hand, gripping it hard as the pain progressed. "There are some herbs in the pack," she told him. "You will have to get some more hot water from the landlord." Joseph looked around bewildered. The pack lay on the floor where he had hurriedly pulled out the sleeping mat and blanket. The pouch with the baby's swaddling cloths lay on top, a pouch with herbs beside it. "Get some hot water," he mumbled to himself.

Thankful to have something to do, he grabbed the jug the servant had brought earlier, hurried away to the inn, and pounded on the locked door. Sleepily the landlord poked his head from an upper window. "Go away," he ordered. "I don't have any more rooms!' His head had almost disappeared before Joseph was able to get his attention again. "My wife is having her baby," he shouted.

The landlord's head popped out through the window again. "Having her baby?" his voice sounded incredulous. "Wife," he thundered as he closed the window, "wake up! We have a young woman giving birth in our barn!"

Things seemed to move swiftly and yet in slow motion as the landlord and his wife answered Joseph's call. Water on the hearth was still warm from the evening's late meals. The landlord's wife brought another jug, some bowls, towels. She piled them into Joseph's arms. "Don't just stand there, young man," she ordered. Bustling through the barnyard, she entered the stall where Mary lay.

Mary's Story

The pains were coming closer together, Mary could tell. She hoped Joseph would come back soon. A strange voice interrupted her concentration of the pain she was trying to keep at bay. The landlord's wife issued orders to the men, who positioned Mary more comfortably for the birth. The herbs were doused in the hot water, and Mary forced herself to drink the bitter concoction. It eased the pain.

"Is there anything more I can do?" Joseph asked.

"You've done your part now," the landlord's wife told him. "Go out and build a bonfire and warm yourself. You won't be sleeping in your bed any more this night."

In the end, it was a quick birth. Three hours of pain and release, then more pain, until Mary thought there would be no end to the pain, and she screamed with the agony at the last push before the baby began to appear.

The landlady's soothing encouragement helped her know what was happening. "I see the baby's head," she said. "It looks healthy."

Hearing the scream, Joseph rushed back into the barn just in time to hear the landlady's words. Another pain racked Mary and another scream pushed the baby out into the landlady's hands. She glanced at Joseph. "Where are the swaddling cloths?"

Joseph grabbed the bag that Mary had so carefully packed. Using one piece of soft cloth, the landlady swabbed the baby clean. She used a knife from the pack to cut the umbilical cord, which she had tied tightly with a piece of flax twine. Wrapping the baby against the chill, she handed him to Joseph and turned her attention back to Mary. Joseph sat holding his son—no, the Messiah of God entrusted to his care—staring into the baby's dark eyes. It seemed no time at all before the landlady took the baby away from him and give him to Mary. "He'll need to nurse soon for strength," she said.

She picked up the things she had used. Joseph cleaned away the bloody straw and opened the second bale. He spread clean straw around Mary and added a good armload to the manger. He unearthed another blanket from the pack, laid it on top of the straw, and stood back to admire his handiwork. "No king could ask for a nicer bed," Mary murmured from her pallet.

Joseph glanced at the landlady. "How can I repay you?" he asked. "I don't know how we would have managed without you."

"It's nice to be needed," she replied. She gathered everything up, piled it in Joseph's arms again, and ushered him back out toward the inn. "Let her rest and nurse the baby now. You can see them both again soon enough," she said.

Mary lay there with the baby. How different the birth of this baby was from the birth of Elizabeth's baby. Elizabeth had two midwives, a clean home, processions of friends and well-wishers, baby gifts; even the priests had come to her home. This baby had none of those things. No friends, no midwives, no gifts. Mary looked around the barn. It wasn't too bad there in that stall, but it certainly wasn't a clean home; it was fairly warm and dry, but it wasn't right.

The Stable

Tears began to fall as she lay there in the straw. She felt she had let God down in bringing this special baby into the world in such a place as a barn. They should have lived in a house. She should have stayed in Nazareth. Maybe, had Mary stayed at home, her mother would have relented and helped her once she went into labor. There were midwives in Nazareth. Surely they would have come and helped her have the baby. It wasn't right, she thought once again, to have the Messiah born in a barn!

The landlord sat by the fire, adding more wood. Joseph took the things toward the inn, where the woman let herself into the kitchen and motioned for him to leave them. Joseph stepped outside, when he began to hear voices. "The angel sent us," one man said excitedly. "We've come to see the baby. We've come to visit the new king of Israel."[2]

---

[2] The story of the shepherds is found in Luke 2:8–18.

Chapter 11

The Shepherds

"What are you talking about?" the landlord growled. "I want to get back to my bed. What do you mean, the new king of Israel?"

"The angels came—" a young boy began to babble. But he was quickly hushed by an older shepherd, who began to explain, "We were out in the hills watching our sheep, when an angel appeared in the sky."

"I have never felt so scared in my life," another man interrupted.

The rest nodded in agreement. "But the angel told us not to be afraid," the shepherd continued. "He said that he was bringing good tidings of great joy to all people. He said the Christ, the Lord, the Messiah, was born here in Bethlehem, that he was wrapped in swaddling cloths and lying in a manger. We hurried from the hills to see him."

"But then there were all the other angels," said another shepherd, taking up the story excitedly. "The sky was filled with them, and they sang a song I had never heard before!"

"Yes," still another voice chimed in. "The words were beautiful. 'Glory to God in the highest, and on earth peace, good will toward men.'"[1]

"They told us about the baby, sang the song, and left," continued the first shepherd. "So we came to Bethlehem to find the baby. If he is not here in your manger, he is in another. There aren't too many mangers in Bethlehem. We are going to find him."

Joseph heard the end of their story. He stepped into the firelight. "He is here," he said. The shepherds surged toward him in unison. "Wait a moment," he said. "I need to see if my wife is all right. Then you may come and see the baby." The men nodded, edging back toward the fire.

Joseph went into the barn. Mary lay on the straw, the baby in her arms. Tears ran down her face. Alarmed, Joseph hurried to her side. "What is wrong, Mary?" he asked. "Do you hurt?"

Mary shook her head and continued to weep.

"Mary!" Exasperation tinged Joseph's voice. "Tell me what is wrong."

"This." Mary waved her hand aimlessly in the air. "This whole thing. This isn't the place for any baby to be born, let alone our special baby. We have let God down, Joseph," she said, gazing at him and her eyes glistening with tears. "When John was born, Elizabeth had everything

---
1 Luke 2:14

The Shepherds

planned so perfectly. She had the midwives, a clean home; they brought the baby gifts. She had nice clothes for the baby. All I have is the swaddling cloth. I don't even have a soft blanket. He has to sleep in a manger."

She gulped back her tears and continued: "People came from all over to visit Elizabeth. The priests came to circumcise John. Everyone brought things for the baby. Everyone was glad to see that baby born. This poor baby doesn't even have grandparents who care about him. Nobody cares that we have this baby but us—and maybe God."

"You're wrong, Mary," Joseph soothed her. "There are many people who care that this baby is born. Someday soon many more people will care. There are people here now to see this special baby of ours."

"What do you mean?" Mary questioned.

"Shepherds—"

"Shepherds! Do you mean to tell me there are shepherds who want to visit my baby?" Incredulity stopped Mary's tears.

"They have been out in the hills watching their sheep, and they hurried to town to see the king of Israel," Joseph said. "Come. Let me put the baby in the manger and then invite the men to see him."

"But how did they know he was here? How did they know he was born? He's just so brand new," said Mary.

"They say angels announced the birth to them," Joseph replied, picking up Jesus and settling him into the manger. "They say there was a whole choir of angels singing about him."

"Angels," Mary breathed, astounded. "Angels have been involved since before the beginning of this baby's life."

Joseph nodded. "The men will tell you all about it when they come in," he assured her. "Are you ready?"

Mary nodded. Pulling the blanket more firmly around her shoulders, she sat up on the sleeping mat and leaned back against the wall of the stall. "I'm ready." The men filed in silently, glanced at Mary, and knelt in front of the manger. "Such a tiny little mite the king is," one remarked reverently.

"He is special, though," answered another quietly. "No angels ever announced the birth of one of my children!"

"Tell me," Mary interrupted them. "Tell me about the angels."

So they repeated the story for her, and one of them sang the song the angels had sung. "Glory to God in the highest, and on earth peace, good will toward men."

"He is the king," another shepherd said. "See, he is dressed just as the angel said he would be and lying in a manger." He shook his head in awe. "Imagine a king being born in a barn."

Mary's Story

Long after the shepherds left, Mary pondered their words.[2] She felt ashamed of herself and her faltering faith in God. She felt ashamed of envying Elizabeth and the wonderful things she had prepared for John. Jesus was much more important than John. Angels had announced his birth. Angels had even sung a special song for him. "Glory to God in the highest," she repeated, "and on earth peace, good will toward men." Exhausted, she lay back down on her sleeping mat. Sometime near dawn Joseph joined her. They slept until the baby cried for his breakfast.

While Mary fed the baby, Joseph set about tidying up the stall. When the baby was fed and clean, Joseph led Mary to the eating area of the inn, where the landlord's wife had prepared a hot meal for them. To Mary's surprise, the shepherds held court in one corner of the room, telling and retelling the story of the angels, the song, and the baby king born in the barn that night. When she and Joseph entered, Jesus in Joseph's arms, they were immediately besieged by well-wishers. Men crowded around to see this baby whose birth had been announced to shepherds by the angels of God.

It took a long time for them to settle again, to allow Mary and Joseph to have their breakfast. One man withdrew from the crowd and approached Joseph. "Where will you be living?" he asked Joseph. "Do you return to your own town?"

Joseph shook his head regretfully.

"There is no reason for us to return," he answered, "at least not soon. Mary needs time to regain her strength, and the baby is too small for such a long journey." He didn't mention that he was unsure how the community would receive Jesus now that he had arrived on the scene.

"I have a house," the man offered. "You are welcome to make it your home while you are in Bethlehem."[3]

"I thank you," Joseph answered. "It will be much better than the landlord's barn, as much as we appreciated its hospitality last night. What is your charge? I haven't much money, but I do have my skills as a carpenter."

"No charge," the man replied. "It's the least I can do for the future king of the nation. Besides, think what revenue I will make when you are gone, and I can say the king lived in my house as a baby." He grinned at Joseph. "If you are a good carpenter, there is plenty of work around here."

Mary, listening to the conversation, dared to hope. If the prophecies were correct, if they were correctly interpreted, she was the mother of the next king of Israel. Hadn't the angel said so when he told her she would have the baby? Hadn't the angel announced it to the shepherds? She heard them excitedly retelling the story as they sat in the corner, regaling each newcomer with the angelic praise, "Glory to God in the highest, and on earth peace, good will to men."

---

2   Luke 2:19
3   Matthew states that Joseph and Mary lived in a house when the Wise Men came (Matt. 2:11). They would not have stayed in the stable for long.

The Shepherds

When they had eaten, Joseph went to settle accounts with the landlord, but the same man waved him aside. "Consider it my gift to the new king." He joined the paean of the shepherds, "and come back and try your skills at some carpentry for me when you're settled in."

So Mary gathered up the baby, Joseph packed up the donkey, and they followed their new landlord to their new home. It wasn't spacious, but it was clean and a definite improvement over the barn with its assorted smells and sounds, and it was much more private than a stall. *It's empty, though*, Mary thought. *Not even a manger to lay Jesus in*. Joseph brought in the packs. He quickly brought out Mary's sleeping mat and blanket so she could lay Jesus down on the floor.

"I'll make him a cradle before anything else," he promised her. She smiled mistily at him. For some reason, this morning she felt very rich.

Chapter 12

Dedication

Joseph was as good as his word. Before the day was over, he had the box of the cradle made. Jesus slept in it that night, and Joseph added rockers the next day. He also worked at the inn and soon became busy with other carpentry jobs. The landlord at the inn and the man who owned their home both spread the word that a good carpenter was in town. A good carpenter wasn't out of work for very long, Mary learned.

Jesus was seven days old when Joseph mentioned that they needed to take him to Jerusalem. "Tomorrow is the eighth day," Joseph reminded Mary. "It is time for his sacrificing and your cleansing. We will go early in the morning to the temple."[1]

Mary agreed. This firstborn son must be dedicated to God with the rites required for the children born to Israel.

After Jesus' 2 a.m. feeding, Mary climbed onto the back of their faithful donkey yet again. Joseph handed her the baby, and they began the ten-mile walk north to Jerusalem. With the earliness of the hour, they would arrive in good time for the afternoon sacrifices. The clopping of the donkey's hooves lulled Jesus back to sleep. Mary wrapped her head covering around the baby to hold him securely and began to doze off herself. Joseph, staff in hand, kept walking.

The temple was busy when they arrived. Pens of sheep, cages of birds, corrals full of the finest cattle Israel boasted were available to buy for sacrifice. Joseph counted out their meager coins. "I can't afford a sheep," he informed Mary. "It will have to be two turtledoves." The law, Mary knew, required a lamb of the first year for a burnt offering and a turtledove for a sin offering.[2] However, if the parents were too poor to afford a lamb, the law allowed them to offer two turtledoves, one for the burnt offering and one for the sin offering.

They looked carefully over the doves available in the cages. Mary wanted to choose the very best they could afford, and Joseph concurred. The Messiah from God deserved the best. He deserved a sheep, Mary thought bitterly. Again she wondered why God didn't make things better for them so they could do this properly. At last they chose a pair of doves, Joseph paid the coins

---

1 Luke 2:21 informs us that Jesus was eight days old when the law required His dedication and circumcision as well as Mary's ritual cleansing. Most commentators agree that He was about forty days old when the Wise Men came to visit and brought their gifts.
2 Leviticus 12:2–8 is the law they followed.

Dedication

the salesman exacted, and they carried the birds into the temple to turn them over to the priests.

They had barely entered the outer court, however, when a man accosted them. "I am Simeon," he informed them. "The Holy Ghost has told me I will not die before I see the Lord's Christ. I am not young. I thought I might not live that long, but now you are here. I have seen the Messiah."[3]

Mary stood open-mouthed as the man spoke. He took the baby from her unresisting arms. "Bless the Lord, oh, my soul;" he repeated the words of the psalmist. "Lord, now let me die in peace as you promised. For I have seen your salvation, which you prepared for all people. A light to enlighten the Gentiles, and the glory of thy people, Israel."

"What does that mean?" Joseph asked.

"This is the Messiah," Simeon replied. Although Mary knew Jesus was the king of Israel, the reference to the Gentiles puzzled her as well as Joseph.

"How did you know we would be here?" she asked.

"The Holy Ghost told me," Simeon replied. He eyed her keenly. "Look, this child is set for the fall and rising again of many in Israel. He is a sign that shall be spoken against." He hesitated as if reluctant to say what followed. "A sword shall pierce your own heart also," he told Mary. "But the life of your child will reveal the thoughts of many hearts."

"Praise the Lord," a woman's voice interrupted Simeon. "I thought I might not live to see this day." She was old, wrinkled. Her voice shook when she spoke. "I am eighty-four years old," she told Mary. "I have lived here in the temple since my husband died, and I was married for only seven years. All these years I have waited for the Messiah. I knew he would come. Now I can tell everyone that I have seen him. Those who have waited for redemption in Israel can rejoice this day."

"What is your name?" Joseph asked her.

"I am Anna, daughter of Phanuel of the tribe of Aser," she replied. "I am a prophetess of the Lord."

One of the priests came out to them at that moment. It was their turn for the sacrifice for Mary's cleansing and the baby's dedication and naming. The priest took the birds, glancing idly at the poor couple and their child. It was a daily, nearly meaningless ritual to him, to name the children of people who should know better than to bring children into a life of poverty. His cynicism left a bad taste in his mouth when he thought of the lives of most of these children had to lead once they left the confines of the temple grounds. Poor people had no right to bear children, in his mind. Never mind the poverty of his own roots. People who couldn't afford even a lamb had no right to bring children into the world to go hungry.

He quickly and efficiently killed the birds for sacrifice, took care of the requirements of the law, and asked for the baby's name to be inscribed in the books. Mary pulled off the covering on

---

[3] Simeon's prophecy is found in Luke 2:25–35, 30. Anna follows Simeon in the Bible record in Luke 2:36–38

Mary's Story

her head and looked at Joseph. He nodded. "Jesus ben Joseph Alpheus," she said clearly.

The priest looked up. He had heard that voice before. He knew it. Just the way she said, "Joseph Alpheus." He had heard that name before. He looked at her keenly. Then he knew. Of course. It was the harlot! The woman he had seen that day so long ago talking with the Roman soldier Panthera. He had never forgotten that. Here was this woman with the Jew she had been engaged to. She had gulled him into claiming her illegitimate child as his own. He knew Joseph to be the carpenter of Nazareth, though, as his sister had told him, they had left Nazareth. Here was a Jewish man with the effrontery to claim a Roman dog as a descendant of Father Abraham.

Bile boiled in his throat. *Not if I can help it*, he thought.[4]

Just to be sure, he asked the mother to repeat the name. "Jesus ben Joseph Alpheus," she said once again.

"And what is your name?" the priest asked Mary. It wasn't customary or usual for a priest to ask the mother's name if the father was present, but she didn't know that.

"Mary, the daughter of Heli of Nazareth," she answered.

Triumph confirmed the priest's suspicions. The daughter of Heli of Nazareth—the girl his sister had engaged to this young carpenter last year. He remembered what his sister had told him of the girl's flightiness, of her lack of proper respect, of her cavalier treatment of the offer this fine young man had made her. He felt a deep sympathy for the man before him for just a moment. One day Joseph would thank him for what he was about to do, he told himself.

Taking the quill in his hand, the priest inscribed the name in the genealogical record: "Jesus ben Panthera. Jesus ibn Maryum." The world would know that this young woman had tried to pass off her illegitimate son as the son of Abraham.

Carefully he schooled his features. "You may go," he told the parents. "It is finished."

Mary breathed a sigh of relief as she left the temple and its requirements. Jesus had been good, but it was time to feed him again, and she needed something to eat herself. She said so to Joseph. He found a stall selling fruits and cheeses and bought some for their meal. They took the donkey away from the temple to the park where, during the Feast of Tabernacles, people set up their tents. There he spread a blanket on the ground, and they sat down to eat their impromptu meal.

"What a strange experience," Mary murmured as she bit into an apricot.

"You mean the prophets?" Joseph asked.

"The prophets ... that priest," Mary answered slowly. "I think I have seen him before."

---

[4] There must be some good reason for this supposed genealogical entry in Jerusalem's records. A Jewish priest certainly would not have wanted to enter the name of a Roman soldier's son as the son of Abraham. The idea that Jesus was a descendant of Abraham was later questioned by the priests. In John 8:13, the priests declared that the words Jesus spoke of Himself were not true, and in John 8:19, they asked where his father was. In John 8:41, they said they were "not born of fornication" (intimating that Jesus was), and in John 8:48, they said to Jesus, "Say we not well that thou art a Samaritan, and hast a devil?"

Dedication

"You have," Joseph replied. "His sister was our matchmaker."

"Oh, yes," Mary acknowledged, taking another bite. Although she couldn't quite shake the feeling of unease, she began to enjoy the bright and warm sun. Jesus demanded her attention. She forgot all about the strangeness of the morning in taking care of the baby's needs. When she and Joseph talked about that day in later years, they remembered not the priest but the prophets, and they often wondered at the meaning of the prophecies they heard that day.

Mary reflected on Simeon's words, "A sword shall pierce your own heart also." But then she remembered the angel's song, "Glory to God in the highest, and on earth peace, good will toward men." She was comforted. God was in control.

Chapter 13

God disperses His religion in ways that many people don't consider. Because of the upheaval and unrest brought on by wars and economics, Jews and their religion had been displaced, and thus had spread, to many parts of the known world by the time Jesus was born. The Scriptures had been translated into what was considered to be the most educated language of the world, Greek, in the third century BC, so by Jesus' birth this translation (called the Septuagint) had already been in existence for 200 years.

Although the main leadership of the Jewish people consisted of the high priest, Sanhedrin, and the scribes of the Jerusalem temple, synagogues stood all over the world as a testimony to the one true God. In Heliopolis, in Egypt, there stood another temple to the true God. Although many Gentiles ridiculed the Jews as a lazy people, giving up not only the seventh day to indolence but also the seventh year, which was incomprehensible, others embraced the religion. The Jewish leaders had erected a series of hoops through which the Gentiles were expected to go before they were considered to be true Jews. They were to agree to circumcision, abstain from eating unclean foods, particularly pork, and agree to baptism by immersion. Impressed by the obvious blessing of their God, by the Jews' prosperity in spite of what some saw as indolence, many proselytes joined the Jewish faith. Among those who read and believed the Jewish scriptures were some of the most important magi of the Eastern world.[1] So sure were they of the prophecies, of the importance of the Jewish Messiah that would be born, that they traveled all over the world to verify the authenticity of any report of that birth. When the story came that the Messiah had been born in Italy, some of the wise men traveled there.

These wise men were also astronomers. They studied the stars. Their Chaldean heritage taught them the importance of the seasons and what would happen when certain planets reached certain places in the heavens. In their studies they realized that the time was right for the Messiah.[2]

Even the Gentiles hoped for a kind of messiah. Wars had ripped the world apart. Thousands of Jews had been killed by the Herods for insurrection or simply to gratify the Herods' lust for

---
1   SDA Bible Commentary, vol. 5, p. 288.
2   There are still astronomers who can point out the conjunction of stars, and explain why it is a symbol of the birth of a king of Judea.

The Magi

blood. The Jewish teaching that the Messiah would bring about a time of peace was a promise the most hardened hoped might come true. The magi could point to a climactic circumstance every 860 years with the conjunction of three planets in the heavens. That, combined with their study of the Scriptures, convinced them the time was ripe.

As some of these wise men continued to study and watch the heavens, they found things changing. Not only were they beginning to see a bright light in the sky at night, different from any other, but they also began having dreams. They became convinced that the Messiah was being born in Judea. As a group they decided to travel to visit this new king. To commemorate his birth, they took with them some of the most costly gifts they could amass, gold (known everywhere for its worth), frankincense, and myrrh. Taken from the barks of trees gown only in the Eastern world, these incenses were important to temple worship and were used in perfumes and for embalming the dead.

Used to traveling long distances on their quests for the Messiah, the men traveled by foot and camel at night. They crossed deserts and rivers and seas to reach their destination, always following the star that beckoned them on.

One morning just before dawn, the star seemed to stop over the temple in Jerusalem. Knowing they were nearly at the end of their quest, the Wise Men stopped just outside Jerusalem to rest and wait for the temple services to begin. They entered the court of the Gentiles early in the morning. Jewish priests worked in the court. As soon as they could get the attention of one of the priests, the Magi asked their all-important question. "Where is he that is born king of the Jews?"

Certainly if anyone knew of a Jewish king, the leaders of Israel would know and support him, they reasoned. The priest whom they asked stared at them in undisguised terror. "There is no king of the Jews," he answered.

"But the prophecies of the Messiah are fulfilled," one of the Magi pointed out. "We have come by camel at night. We have crossed deserts and rivers and seas to reach our destination, always following the star that beckoned us on."

"There are many self-appointed messiahs," the priest answered. "The latest I know of calls himself Simon Judas. He lives up north, near Nazareth. There have been rumors of the Messiah's arrival all my life."

The men from the East looked at each other in consternation. "Perhaps if we talked with a scribe," one suggested, "or one of the priests higher in office, they could—"

"There is no time for the scribes to visit with you now," the priest interrupted contemptuously. "This is the busy part of the morning. All the priests are busy with the sacrifices. This is not a good time of day for you to even be here." He dismissed them as unworthy. How could these Gentiles be given the understanding of when the Messiah was to be born? There were priests and scribes who should know more then they did. His disdain flicked them like a whip, but in the back of his eyes they noted another emotion—stark fear.

Making their way from the temple grounds, the Magi conferred among themselves. "What shall we do? Where will we find what we are searching for?" they questioned. Had it been Passover, when Orthodox Jews and their proselytes traveled to Jerusalem from all over the world, the presence of these men from the East in the midst of a great pilgrimage may have gone unnoticed. But their questions, their appearance, were noted by everyone in the court of the Gentiles. As they made their way out of the court, they decided to approach more people with their question. It wasn't unreasonable that the current ruling power simply did not know about a new king. It wasn't the first time in history that a king had been born unknown, unnamed. *What of the important kings of the past?* they reasoned. The first king of Israel, Saul, was virtually unknown before Samuel had anointed him; and then David was no more than a shepherd boy. They knew they couldn't be wrong. Their studies, the star, the attitude of the priest, all seemed to point to a king.

A man who had been in the court of the Gentiles stepped up to the men from the East. "I overheard your question," he said. "Are you sure the Messiah is born?"

"We are sure," they answered.

The man, uninhibited joy in his face, began to shout, "Do you hear this? The Messiah is born! These men have been led of God to come here and find him!"

A crowd gathered as the man began to shout the message again. Those in the priesthood may not be pleased with the news, the Magi realized, but the masses were still waiting for release from their bondage to a foreign government. The priest the Magi had seen in the temple came out. Shouldering his way through the crowd, the priest confronted the men from the East.

"What are you doing?" he barked. "Trying to start a riot?"

"We are trying to get the information we seek," they replied.

The priest turned to the crowd. "Do you so easily forget the power of Herod?" he cried.[3] "Disperse before the soldiers come and kill us all. And you," he eyed the Magi balefully, "you take your questions and leave Jerusalem. I hate to think what will happen if Herod should hear that you are asking about another king. He has already killed every member of his own family who could possibly take his throne."

The priest animatedly waved his hands. "Disperse! Quickly!" he ordered. "Don't talk of this openly. Go! Now!" The crowd began to disperse as the priest commanded, hurried on by his reminders of their fears. But as they left, they talked about the question the Magi had raised. Where was the Messiah? Some were elated at the possibility that a Messiah was born. Others, aware of Herod's reputation, warned that this would be just one more reason for a wholesale slaughter of the Jews. This sentiment was echoed throughout Jerusalem as word spread of the

---

3 Herod killed indiscriminately by the thousands. All the incentive his soldiers needed to "keep the peace" was the possibility of a riot. They often quelled these civil disturbances by killing the perpetrator.

The Magi

visitors from the East.[4]

Word reached the high priest through a messenger from Herod. His spies had already informed him of the strange request of the men who had entered town just that morning. "You are expected to present yourselves to Herod immediately," the messenger said. "Bring your books of prophecy."[5]

So the priests obeyed. The high priest whom Herod had placed and replaced in power, the leaders of the twenty-four, and the scribes took all the scrolls of prophecy and entered Herod's palace not without fear. As they entered the audience chamber, Herod paced nervously across the room.

"What do you know about a king of the Jews?" he demanded.

The priests glanced nervously at each other. The answer was obvious, but they dared not tell Herod. "Speak up!" Herod shouted. "You have foreigners who don't even claim to be of your nation coming here asking to see your king. They don't mean me! They want a baby, a newborn! Where is this baby to be born?"

Again the priests and scribes exchanged glances. "In Bethlehem of Judea," one replied.

"How do you know this?"

"The prophet said so," answered one of the scribes. "And thou Bethlehem, in the land of Juda, art not the least among the princes of Juda; for out of thee shall come a Governor that shall rule my people Israel."[6]

"You may go." Herod waved a ring-clad hand dismissively.

Without waiting for further instructions, the priests scurried out of the palace. They placed some distance between themselves and the palace before beginning to discuss the problem. "Why would God tell some Gentile dogs what He will not reveal to us, His priests?" one asked.

"There's nothing to it," another priest replied. "People have been looking for a messiah for years. This is just another of those chases, by Magi. Why, I heard last year some of them went haring off to Italy. As if the Messiah of the Jews would be born in Italy! These have just figured out that the Jewish Messiah must be born a Jew!"

A nervous laugh followed that sally.

"There's nothing to it," a priest said. Most of them nodded in agreement.

"There's nothing to it, but Herod bears watching," another warned.

The Wise Men, sitting under the trees in the tenting area, watched the priests leave Herod's palace. The men looked nervous at first, but by the time they reached the temple itself just a few blocks away, they were laughing among themselves. So intent was their attention on the priests, they didn't notice another figure leave the palace.

---

4   The *SDA Bible Commentary*, vol. 5, p. 290.
5   See Matt. 2:4
6   Matt. 2:6

"Herod wishes to see you," the messenger said as he reached the Wise Men.[7]

They stirred. Leaving packs and animals with their servants, they followed the man to the palace. Herod was still pacing, the messenger saw, but he stopped and indicated the visitors should be seated. "Tell me," he inquired pleasantly, "what brought you here asking about the Jewish king."

"We have seen his star in the East." they replied.

"Describe it," Herod ordered.

The Wise Men did what they were told. "We might not have understood its significance had we not also had dreams," one said.

"How long ago did the star appear?" Herod asked.

"We have been studying it for nearly a year," they replied. "It appeared late winter or early spring." They conferred a bit together. "Yes, early spring," they concluded. Herod pointed the forefingers of both hands together against his chin, turned his back, and paced several steps. Abruptly he turned back toward them as if having made a weighty decision.

"Go to Bethlehem. That is where I am informed the baby is to be born," he told them. "Go and search. Don't stop searching, even if you have to turn the whole town upside down. When you have found the baby, don't tell anyone else. Come and tell me. I wish to go and worship him with you."

The Wise Men bowed. Turning, they made their way from the palace and to the camping area, where they rested until the sun made its nightly vigil on the western horizon. Then they saddled their pack animals, including the sleeping mats they had taken out to rest on during the day, and began the last leg of their journey by night to find the new king.

As they left behind the outskirts of the city of Jerusalem, they felt a burden lift. "How can anyone live under the intrigue that abounds in that place?" one asked.

"I couldn't," another exclaimed.

"Look! There's the star!"

Very early in the morning, the star stopped. It dipped down and settled over the roof of a humble house in the heart of Bethlehem. The men following it had no choice but to stop as well. "Can this be the birthplace of a king?" they asked one another.[8]

But they had followed the star for over 400 miles. There was no place else to go. Settling themselves for the remainder of the night, they waited for morning when the inhabitants of the house would waken.

Mary, caring for Jesus' early morning feeding, glanced out the window. Shadows covered the yard in front of the house and spilled out into the street. Some of them moved. Moving quickly and quietly, she awoke Joseph.

---

7   See Matt. 2:7, 8
8   The whole story of the Magi is found in Matt. 2:1–12.

The Magi

"There's something strange outside. And there's a strange light. I haven't seen anything quite like it before," she told him.

Immediately alert, Joseph rose from his sleeping mat and hurried to the window. In the dim light he could see the shadows of pack animals, camels, it seemed. On the ground a group of men obviously slept.

"Take the baby to the back of the house," Joseph whispered cautiously. "I'm going to see what this is."

"Be careful, Joseph," Mary warned, clutching his sleeve.

Joseph patted her hand comfortingly. "I will."

Advancing cautiously, Joseph let himself out of the house. The light was brighter now, not unlike the full of the moon, but there was no moon. And the light seemed to come from the house. Joseph turned. An involuntary gasp escaped him at the sight of the bright star seeming to hover over the roof of the house.

"Beautiful, isn't it?" a voice spoke behind him. "We have followed that star for more than 400 miles to find this place. Do you live within?"

Joseph whirled to face a tall Eastern stranger.

"Who are you?" he croaked. "What do you want here?"

Their voices woke up the other sleeping men, who rose to stand behind the first. Joseph considered his foolishness in coming out without even his staff.

"We have came from the East," the man spoke out of the night. "We are magi, wise men. We have studied the heavens and the prophecies and were given dreams. We have come to pay homage to the king of the Jews. Is he within?"

Nothing in Joseph's wildest dreams had prepared him for that moment; but then, he reflected, nothing in his life had prepared him for the experiences he had had during the last eight months. Catching his breath, he replied evenly, "He is here."

The group of men let out a cheer. "At last!" one replied. Immediately they went to their pack animals. As they busied themselves getting something from their packs, Joseph stepped to the door of the house. "Mary," he called quietly. "Come out here."

Stepping out of the door with Jesus in her arms, Mary noticed the change in the light as Joseph had. He reached for her hand, squeezing it comfortingly, as he drew her further away from the house. Then, placing his hand on her shoulder, Joseph turned her toward the house. Her reaction was all he could have hoped for. "What a glorious sight," she breathed, "But what does it mean?"

She looked again at Joseph and then remembered the men. "What do they want?"

"They want to pay homage to Jesus," Joseph replied. "They want to worship your son."

"They what?"

"They want to pay homage to the king of the Jews."

Mary's Story

Mary gasped. She should not have been surprised, she supposed, but these men weren't humble shepherds. She looked at them more closely. These were some of the best educated men in the world. Everyone knew Eastern wise men were always learning. And she had no doubt as to who they were.

"Go light a lamp," Joseph urged her, "and settle Jesus in his cradle. I'm sure no king ever had more distinguished guests."[9]

"I have nothing to offer them in the way of refreshments," Mary protested.

"I doubt that matters," Joseph answered.

Mary had barely settled Jesus in his cradle and lit the lamp when the men entered the house with Joseph. Their arms were full of gifts. Carefully each one stepped up to the cradle where Jesus lay.

Each man laid his gift on the floor by the baby's bed, then stepped back, knelt, and put his head to the floor in abject obeisance. Mary stood in absolute amazement. Of course she knew her baby was special; he was a special gift from God. But seeing these men, these Gentiles, worship her son as God Himself thrilled her. She wasn't sure what it meant.

The men didn't stay long. *They can't carry on a conversation with a king who wasn't yet old enough to stay awake for the whole ceremony,* Mary thought ruefully, as Jesus, sleepy and full, closed his eyes and slept before the last man had laid his gifts on the floor.

Joseph followed them out. Mary took the lamp and went to move the gifts the men had brought to another place. There were so many things piled around the cradle, she couldn't get to the baby to take care of him. As she began to move them, she gasped. Piled around her baby were the most beautiful containers she had ever seen filled with the most costly gifts in the world: gold, frankincense, and myrrh. Joseph entered as she placed the last container on the table.

"Do you know what they left here?" she asked in a slightly strangled voice.

"No."

"Look." Mary gestured at the gifts that literally covered the table before her.

Joseph looked. "Good" was all he said. Hoof beats sounded outside as the men rode away.

"They are leaving already?" Mary asked. "They told me they were to go to Jerusalem and report to Herod where we are," Joseph answered her. "But they saw an angel appear to them in a dream who told them to go home another way. They are wasting no time. They are going back where they came from."[10]

Joseph gave her a keen look. "Come, let's get a little more sleep before morning." Thankful Jesus was sleeping well, Mary turned to go back to bed. As she glanced out of the window, she

---

9   The idea of only three Wise Men originates from the numeration of three gifts. There is no record as to how many men there were, and they would likely have traveled with servants and bodyguards. It must have been a startling sight to Mary and Joseph to be visited by these dignitaries from the East, whom everyone knew to be brilliant scholars.

10 See Matt. 2:12

noticed the deeper darkness. "The star; it's gone," she said wistfully.

"That's good," Joseph answered. "Had the star stayed, Herod would certainly find Jesus. It left while the Wise Men were worshiping Jesus."

They settled back on their sleeping mat. Joseph wrapped his arms about Mary and soon settled into his usual snore. Mary lay awake for quite a while thinking of all that had happened that night. She had barely closed her eyes, finally falling sleep, it seemed, when Joseph was shaking her awake again.

"Get up, Mary," he said urgently. "We have to leave right now. An angel came to me in a dream and warned me. Herod will not wait. He intends to kill Jesus. We are to go to Egypt without delay."

As soon as he saw she was fully awake, Joseph grabbed the pack bags. He put his tools in one, the gifts from the Wise Men in another, and tossed yet another to Mary for clothes. "Hurry," he urged.

Even when they left Nazareth, Mary had not packed as quickly as she packed that early morning. Food stores that would not keep she threw out. Those they could take with them to eat on the way she piled into a pack bag. Clothes and sleeping mats filled another. Joseph came rushing in. "Are they ready?" he asked. She nodded, handing him the clothes first, then the food. He took them and lashed them to the faithful donkey. Then he rushed in, picked up Jesus, cradle and all, and set him on top of the donkey's load. Tying the cradle carefully, he made a safe place for the baby to ride.

Mary took the candle and made a frantic tour of the house, making sure they were leaving nothing behind. Then she wrapped her cloak about her and joined Joseph in the yard. The sun was graying the sky as they began to walk without saying a word. They had cleared the outskirts of town before Mary observed, "It will take us very long to reach Egypt if we walk all the way."

"I'll buy some horses at the first place we find some for sale," Joseph promised.

"All right," Mary agreed. They continued walking in silence. For the second time, Mary was leaving everything behind for the sake of her son.

V

Egypt

Chapter 14

Flight in the Night

True to his word, Joseph purchased four strong horses just outside Hebron. He traded the donkey, remarking that a pack horse would do better at keeping up during the journey ahead of them. Mary was sorry to see the faithful animal go, but it had been a long, hard day of walking before they reached that town, and she knew Joseph was right

They found a good camping place. Then Joseph went back to town to find some supplies, more food, fabric for the baby's swaddling cloths, burnooses for the hot desert they were about to cross. When Jesus fussed, Mary took time to stop and feed and change him. She felt nervous with Joseph gone and watched the trail behind them for Herod's soldiers, but she never saw them.

Joseph had stayed away from the main camping areas. He didn't want anyone to take word of their whereabouts back to the king. The angel had impressed him mightily as to how important it was to keep Jesus safe from that man's wicked plans to kill the baby.

The next morning Joseph saddled two of the horses, piled the packs on the backs of the other two, and helped Mary into the saddle. "Do you know how to ride a horse?" Joseph asked, a little concerned.

Mary smiled. "It can't be much harder than riding a donkey, can it?" she asked in turn.

"Stronger, though. More high-spirited. And I won't be leading her." Joseph frowned a bit. "You'll have to hold her in check." He patted the mare's cheek as he spoke. "She's well broken, though. You shouldn't have any trouble, but I'll carry the baby with me until I'm sure you can handle the horse."

Mary nodded. Her nerves felt tight with excitement and fear. Joseph kicked his mount's flanks, and Mary followed suit. They were ready to ride.

They rode hard all day. When they saw a caravan coming to meet them, Joseph veered off into the desert, skirting the trail until the caravan was well past, so as not to be noticed and perhaps reported. They stopped at regular intervals to feed and change Jesus as well as eat and drink a little themselves.

Mary's Story

Late in the afternoon they bypassed the town of Beersheba.[1] The last outpost of Israeli civilization lay behind them now. They camped that night where the rivers forked, where the Thameil and es Seba joined to make the larger stream of the Gaza River. Because they were less likely to meet travelers there, Joseph knew this would be the best place to cross. Most of the other travelers would cross the river at the ford. He also took time to fill the water skins. They faced forty miles through the Wilderness of Sin before they reached more water at the River of Egypt.[2]

Wearily Mary unpacked the food, took care of Jesus, lay out the sleeping mats, and ate a little. Joseph unloaded the pack horses, took off the saddles, and tied the animals for the night.

"You must eat more," Joseph encouraged her. "You must keep up your strength."

"I haven't much strength to keep up," Mary protested, rubbing her backside. The horse's saddle had felt much more comfortable early in the morning than it did now. She wondered if she could force herself to ride again the next day. Joseph had traveled hard, and she knew they would travel hard again. He would not rest easy until they had crossed the border into Egypt.

"How far will we go tomorrow?" Mary asked, hoping it wouldn't be such a grueling ride.

"It will be another hard day." Joseph looked at her compassionately. "We might make the River of Egypt if we could ride harder and faster than today, but it's desert all the way. It would be easier if Jesus were not so small." He shrugged. "We have enough water for a dry camp if we need to. We will likely camp halfway. Thirty or forty miles tomorrow, and the rest the following day."

"Will we be in Egypt when we cross the river?"

"No," Joseph replied slowly. "I understand it's better than sixty miles across the Wilderness of Shur before we reach the Red Sea. When we cross that, we will really be in Egypt. We're always safe, Mary." Joseph wrapped his arm around her shoulders and squeezed. "God is protecting us."

"But He won't protect us if we don't obey Him," Mary said.

"Which is exactly what we are doing traveling this road tonight," Joseph pointed out. "Let's sleep. Morning will be here before you know it."

Mary felt a little better the next morning. She ate more food, drank a lot more. She knew Joseph would travel hard again. He would not rest easy until they had crossed the border into Egypt.

In the end, because of the heat of the day and the hard going for the horses through the sand, they spent three days crossing the wilderness. Mary found herself remembering the stories

---

1   An ancient town in Palestine, Beersheba was home to Abraham, Jacob, and the post-exiled Jews. It was also a "safe" town where a man could run for his life if accused of a crime. Except for Kadesh-bamea, which at the time of Christ was no longer inhabited, it shared the distinction with Dan of being the southernmost town in the kingdom.

2   There were two distinct wilderness areas in the northern area of the Sinai peninsula. Dry desert divided about one-third of the way by the River (or Creek) of Egypt. Perhaps in drier years, it was no more than a depression in the sand with no water at all.

Flight in the Night

her parents had told her of when the Israelites had crossed those wildernesses 1,000 years ago.[3] They said God had given their ancestors a pillar of fire by night and a pillar of cloud by day. Mary envied them. The cloud would keep the sun off them, and the fire at night would certainly feel good. Temperatures at night dropped low, and dew always soaked their blankets by morning. Joseph loaded the sleeping mats and blankets on top of the horses to dry.

Toward midday, they wished the blankets had stayed damp. The sun burned hot around them, and even with the loose-fitting desert clothes and headdresses, Mary felt she would faint from the heat. They stopped when the sun got too hot, in the dubious shade of rocks, and drank water and rested the horses. As soon as it cooled, they went on traveling until it was nearly too dark to make camp. Joseph took time during the hot part of the day to scout firewood for the campfire at night, loading it on top of the patient pack horses. In the cool of the desert evening, the fire was welcome.

Late in the afternoon of the third day, the horses raised their heads, sniffed the air, and speeded their gait. Mary looked up. Along the horizon she saw trees. At first she dismissed them as another mirage, but as they drew closer, she realized she was seeing the oasis along the banks of the river. They had made it; they had crossed the Wilderness of Sin.

"Look, Joseph," she called. "The river."

"I see it," he replied. Though his voice was calm, she sensed the underlying excitement in him. They were there. If they had made it through one wilderness, they would make it through another.

As he unloaded the pack, Joseph carefully took out the menorah and candles, the specially embroidered cloths they sat upon, and arranged them on a rock. When Mary came back from washing in the river, she exclaimed, "Why, Joseph. Why did you do that?"

"It's Preparation Day," Joseph replied calmly.

"Why, so it is. How forgetful of me. Traveling, I guess I lost track of the days."

"We'll stay here tomorrow," Joseph decreed, "and keep the Sabbath rest in this place."

Mary instinctively glanced the way they had come across the desert. "What about Herod?"

"God doesn't want us to desecrate the Sabbath," Joseph replied firmly, "even for fear of Herod. He will protect us, Mary."

"You're right," Mary replied. She wondered if she had begun to rely more on Joseph than on God, that Joseph had to remind her of it.

They spent a peaceful Sabbath on the shores of the River of Egypt and prepared to leave at daybreak on the first day of the week. Mary dreaded the trip through the Wilderness of Shur. It was twice as far, twice as dry, and twice as bad, but they had to travel through it to reach Egypt,

---

3   "And the Lord went before them by day in a pillar of cloud, to lead them the way; and by night in a pillar of fire, to give them light; to go by day and night; He took not away the pillar of the cloud by day, nor the pillar of fire by night from before the people" (Exod. 13:21, 22).

Mary's Story

so she climbed into her saddle without comment. Joseph handed Jesus up to her, gripped the reins of the pack animals and climbed aboard his own mount. They made the ford safely and were soon beyond the cool confines of the river.

Joseph pushed them hard. Mary knew he was hoping to be in Succoth before the next Preparation Day. He had some family there, who would take them in. Then, he told her, he wanted to go on to Heliopolis. There was a temple in Heliopolis and more Israelites and probably plenty of carpentry work. Even so, they stopped frequently to feed Jesus, let the animals rest, and rested themselves during the hot part of the day.

The nights remained cold, and dew wet their wool blankets early, waking them to the new day. It was good to get an early start. They could travel longer before the heat stopped them again. As soon as the sun lowered and the heat cooled, they mounted up and traveled until it was nearly too dark to see. Occasional caravans passed them, but now Joseph didn't avoid them. There were others traveling on the road to Egypt, and their passing seemed less remarkable.

The morning of the fifth day, Joseph opened the last water skin. "We'll have to be conservative with our water from here on," he remarked. He measured some water for the horses carefully and handed Mary a cupful to drink. "Perhaps today we will sleep during the hot part of the day and travel in the dark until we are too tired to go farther," he remarked.

While Mary dreaded the extra miles, she agreed with him. They needed to conserve as much of the water as possible, and the night travel would make it easier on the horses. When it got hot, Joseph found some scant shade near some rocks, laid out the sleeping mats and, after they ate, they lay down to sleep. The heat wasn't the best thing to sleep in, Mary reflected, as she tossed fitfully on her mat. She wished for cool water to wash with, but there wasn't enough.

At last the sun began to slide town the western sky, the air became a little cooler. Joseph watered the animals, gave Mary a drink, and packed up, ready to move on. They rode late that night, thankful for the light of a full moon.

At sunset Joseph loosened the blankets from the packs and wrapped one around Mary and the baby. He kept one for himself. The wool warded off the chill until the moon went down and there was no light to guide their way. Then Joseph built a fire to keep the wild animals at bay.

The next morning, they had traveled only a short distance before they met a well-loaded caravan. "How far is it to Succoth," Joseph asked the leader of the group.

"You travel there, do you?" the man queried.

"Indeed," Joseph answered.

"You do well," the man said. "You should reach Succoth soon. It is only about twenty-five more miles. But you will want to be there in time for the ferry across the Red Sea."

He smiled at Mary, then noticed the baby. "What have we here?" he asked.

"Our son, Jesus," Mary replied softly. She pulled the wraps away from Jesus' face.

Moved, the man pulled a package from his pack. "For the baby," he said gruffly. Joseph

Flight in the Night

reached for his purse to pay the man, but he waved him away. "No, that baby is special," the man said.

Knowing how close they were to their destination, Joseph and Mary pressed on, not stopping even though it got hot. They ate dried fruit and nuts from the packs and pushed their mounts onward. Soon they saw the first trees near the sea. Fresh vigor seemed to move through the horses as they smelled the water. Now they didn't need to urge their mounts. The water beckoned them all.

The ferry was still on their side of the sea when they arrived. Joseph talked to the man in charge, paid him the required coins, and carefully loaded the animals on the boat. Soon the sails were unfurled, and they began to move across the water. It seemed to take a very long time to reach the other side. They still had miles to go before they reached Succoth. It was nearly dark when they got there.

Joseph asked for directions to the Jewish synagogue, and they hurried through the streets, knowing that a priest would be able to tell them where Joseph's relatives lived. They expected most people to be at home celebrating the coming of the Sabbath, and they were surprised to find a crowd gathered in the synagogue when they arrived. People were weeping. It looked like a funeral, but they saw no bier.

"What is happening?" Joseph stopped one man to ask.

"Did you just arrive here?" the man asked in return.

At Joseph's nod of affirmation, the man answered. "Then you wouldn't have heard. We just received a message that Herod has killed all the boy children under two years of age in Bethlehem."[4] The man seemed to gulp for air, then continued. "My brother's firstborn son was one of those killed. Excuse me." He hurried away.

---

[4] See Matt. 2:16, 17

Chapter 15

The Slaughter of the Innocents

Joseph looked at Mary. Her face was drawn and white. Fear turned her eyes into large dark orbs as she stared back at him. "It's because of Jesus. Because the Wise Men went to Herod first," she whispered. "Oh, those poor mothers!" Tears filled her eyes.

Mary remembered the words of the prophet Simeon in the temple. She hadn't understood his prophecy, "A sword shall pierce your own heart also." *Is this what he meant?* Her heart ached for those mothers deprived of their children. She felt almost responsible for their babies' deaths. Those swords depriving those children of life were meant for Jesus. *Was that why the angel had warned us? Why didn't the angel warn everyone in Bethlehem?* There was so much Mary wished she had answers for.

That Sabbath was one of mourning throughout the Jewish community. As they got better acquainted with the others living in Succoth, Mary and Joseph heard more details. They were told how the soldiers of Herod had gone to every house in town. They had come in legions covering the town quickly. There had been no time to warn anyone, no time to hide baby boys. They had ripped the swaddling cloths off every infant under two years old they could find. Girls they left naked in their screaming mothers' arms; boys they ran through with swords, seeming to delight in their butchery.

More horror stories surfaced in the weeks that followed as travelers from Bethlehem carried with them news of the raid and slaughter. The gruesome death the boys were subjected to was in many cases turned into a horrific spectacle; this atrocity was tragic and heartbreaking to a degree that words fail to express. It was said that the soldiers dragged some of the babies through the streets at the end of ropes.

Each story wrenched Mary's heart anew. While she was thankful for Jesus' safety, she hurt for every mother whose child had been destroyed. She reflected on the ability of men to be so cruel, and she remembered the soldier Panthera, who had helped her reach Elizabeth's house. Had he been one of those assigned to kill the babies? She hoped not. He had been such a good man. He had been so concerned that her baby be safe. She didn't think he could kill babies, but he was a soldier of Herod, and he would do what he was commanded to do, she knew.

As each new messenger arrived, Mary and Joseph, along with others in the community,

The Slaughter of the Innocents

waited to hear that the slaughter had spread to other towns, but no such news arrived. It seemed that Herod had vented his wrath on one small town and that he wanted no more blood from Jewish children. Mary was thankful for that. But it confirmed her belief that Herod had been trying to kill her baby when he had ordered the slaughter of the innocent babies of Bethlehem. That's what people were calling it, the Slaughter of the Innocents.

People began saying that they could expect no less of a man who had murdered a thousand Jewish men in one day in the temple courtyard. They recalled that Herod had also murdered his own children.

It was common knowledge that Herod had five wives.[1] Doris, an Idumaean from south of Judea was the first and one whom he later divorced. He then married Mariamne, the granddaughter of Hyrcanus II, high priest and king of Judea. Herod killed Hyrcanus shortly after his marriage to Mariamne. Everyone knew it was because the old priest and king had tried to turn Herod back to the true God. Herod killed Mariamne the year following her grandfather's death because she had dared to name her sons after her Jewish grandfathers, Aristobulus and Alexander, rather than call them Herods. Most people thought Herod was afraid he would lose his throne to these two children, who had more right to the Jewish throne than he did because of their grandfather's kingship.

Educated in Rome, Aristobulus and Alexander were handsome men and were proud of their royal heritage. As grandsons of the last ruling Jewish king, Antigonus, they were also proud of their connections with Hyrcanus II, Antigonus' father. Their popularity with the Jews made them ideal candidates for overthrowing their father's government, which most people felt was too expensive. Herod's taxes were, most people believed, excessive, and these sons supported that belief. They promised a better kingdom. They certainly had the support of prominent Jews in their bid for their father's throne, as well as support from Antipater and their aunt Salome, Herod's sister. The boys were in their early twenties, people recalled, when Herod had them killed.[2] At the same time he condemned these sons to die, Herod ordered the assassination of 300 Jewish leaders who were known to have supported Aristobulus and Alexander.[3]

Those who were not of that lineage, those whose mothers had the sense to name their children after Herod's own ancestors, were spared. It was a well-known fact that Herod tried to deny his own Jewish roots, trying to curry favor with the ruling Roman powers. For that, as much as his cruelty, Jews everywhere despised him.

Fear did strange things to people, Mary mused, *but it was obvious that Herod had been afraid of his children's lineage.*

---

1   Commentators say there were five more wives whose names are unknown or disputed, for a total of ten wives. We have the names of the five referenced in these paragraphs. Herod killed Mariamne and her sons because they belonged to the original ruling class of Maccabean Jews who opposed his ascension to the throne of Judea.
2   *The SDA Bible Commentary*, vol. 5, p. 41.
3   *The SDA Bible Commentary*, vol. 5, p. 42.

Mary's Story

Only three years after Herod assassinated Mariamne's sons, Doris' son Antipater became the third of Herod's children to die from his father's wrath, allegedly because he had attempted to assassinate his father.

Herod's third wife, Malthace, was a Samaritan. Perhaps it was the knowledge that Malthace's heritage enraged the Jews that gave Herod the idea to name her children, Archelaus and Herod Antipas, his heirs. He also married Cleopatra of Jerusalem and Mariamne II, the daughter of Simon, a high priest, probably one put into power by Herod. Both women had sons they named Herod Phillip. Mariamne's son married Herodias, his niece and daughter of the slain Aristobulus. Cleopatra's son married his niece, his brother Herod Phillip's and Herodias' daughter, Salome. No one could blame him. She was by far the most beautiful and attractive of all the ladies in the kingdom.

All of this history the Jews remembered and repeated along with the story of the murdered babies. Of all the cruelties Herod was guilty of, the frivolous, impulsive, and heinous murder of those innocent Jewish children rankled the most. Jews didn't forgive Herod easily for those deaths. The death of the babies added to their hatred for the Jewish ruler turned pagan.

Although Mary and Joseph felt safe from Herod's designs against Jesus at Succoth, they felt the need to go elsewhere for Joseph to find more work. The money from the Wise Men could not last forever. Consequently, a few short weeks after their arrival at Succoth, they repacked the horses and moved on, heading for Heliopolis, their original destination. One day's ride brought them to the Nile River. They camped on its banks, and the next day found them riding into the busy metropolis. It didn't take long to find a house and work. The weeks passed quickly as they settled into their new surroundings. They found it a joy to live closer to a temple and participate in the services there.

They also found it easier to buy copies of the Scriptures, the Talmud, and other writings in Heliopolis than in Jerusalem. These scrolls Joseph packed carefully among their belongings.

Jesus was growing fast. Mary loved to watch his development. They almost forgot at times that Jesus wasn't just their special boy. It was easy to forget that he had a special purpose when he needed the same everyday love, care, and instruction as did any other boy. They were reminded abruptly one early fall night when the angel Gabriel once again visited Joseph in a dream.

"Arise. Take the young child and his mother, and go to the land of Israel, for they are dead which sought the young child's life."[4] Joseph wasn't sure he had heard correctly. But he was now nearly awake, and the angel repeated the message, "Arise. Take the young child and his mother, and go to the land of Israel, for they are dead which sought the young child's life."

The morning was early, but Joseph woke Mary up. "The angel was here," he said softly.

Fear filled Mary's eyes. Joseph hastened to comfort her. "He said Herod is dead. We are to return to Israel."

---

4   Matt. 2:20

The Slaughter of the Innocents

"Now? Why not just stay here a while longer?"

"We are to return to Israel," Joseph said adamantly. "The prophets wrote," he went on almost to himself, "Out of Egypt I have called my son."[5]

---
[5] Matt. 2:15, cf. Hos. 11:1

Chapter 16

Going Home Again

Once again Mary found herself packing up all her belongings. At last everything was ready to go, except Jesus' cradle and their sleeping mats. She had become quite expert at leaving in a hurry, Mary thought almost sarcastically. She dreaded having to make the trip across the wildernesses again. *But,* she thought, *it will be nice to go back to Bethlehem. Things were comfortable there. I have good memories of Bethlehem.*

Joseph came in the house and carried the packs out to the patient horses. Strapping everything in place with minimal effort, Mary noted that Joseph was as expert as she was at moving quickly. They left that afternoon, camping as before on the banks of the Nile before going to Succoth the next day. They wasted little time in that town, simply buying a few provisions for the trip and taking time to fill the water skins from the river. The next morning they faced the desert again.

The days ran together as they traveled. Each day was the same as the day before, traveling before dawn, resting and gathering firewood in the heat of the day, traveling on into the night, until they stopped to build a fire to keep the wild animals at bay and to heat a little food. They dropped bone-weary onto their sleeping mats and woke only to the coldness of the early morning dew soaking the blankets. Joseph always built a morning fire so they could have something warm to eat before they started out. Again they spread the wet blankets on top of the loads to dry as they traveled.

Jesus was more awake on the trip back through the wilderness than he had been on the way out, but he still took two naps each day, and they made good time while he slept in the cradle on top of one of the horses.

At the end of the week they had reached the River of Egypt. Again they crossed the ford to camp on the far side and prepare for the Sabbath. Joseph got out the menorah and the scrolls he had bought in Heliopolis, and they celebrated the Sabbath in nature almost as the first parents had done in the Garden of Eden, except that they were surrounded by other travelers and caravans coming and going. A few other Jews had traveled one way or the other, and they joined Joseph and Mary and the baby in worshiping God on the Holy Day.

Early in the morning on first day of the week they resumed their journey. Mary felt tougher,

Going Home Again

more in tune with her mount, more able to do the long stretches of the journey without fatigue. She had come to almost enjoy the long rides through the wilderness, the varied hues of the sand and rocks, and the occasional lizard, homed toad, or other creature she happened to see.

This trip was much happier than the trip to Egypt had been; Mary knew her destination. She knew what awaited her in Bethlehem. She looked forward to seeing the friends she had made there before the angel sent them to Egypt.

Late in the third day, they rode into Beersheba. Since they were not in such a hurry, Joseph decided they could stop and visit Zacharias and Elizabeth and little John. It was a fortuitous decision, one that would again be a crossroad in their lives.

"Shalom," Joseph called at the doorway. Zacharias met them at the door.

"Shalom yourself," he called. "Elizabeth, see who is here." Elizabeth, baby John on her hip, hurried to greet them. Mary slid expertly from her horse, reached up for Jesus, then hurried to give Elizabeth a one-armed hug.

"But where have you been. How well you've come up in the world, to own four fine horses," Zacharias said, admiring their animals. "Come. Let me help you put them up in the barn, then you will stay for the evening meal and the night and tell us all about what has happened to you."

Elizabeth and Mary entered the house as the men led the horses to the barn. "Come. Tell me, how did you become such an expert horse rider," Elizabeth exclaimed.

"We have been in Egypt," Mary replied.

Elizabeth stopped and stared at Mary in stunned surprise. "Egypt! And here I thought you well-established in Nazareth all this time!" She eyed Mary speculatively. "What do your parents say about your gallivanting off to Egypt?"

"Nothing," Mary replied.

"Nothing? Not even when you took the baby?"

"They haven't even seen the baby." Mary admitted.

Flabbergasted, Elizabeth stared at her cousin. "What do you mean? Surely your mother was present at the birth of her grandson!"

"Didn't Zacharias tell you? My parents disowned me," Mary reminded her.

"Anna was always the stubborn one," Elizabeth said slowly, "but in spite of Zacharias' story, I didn't believe she would really have nothing to do with her only daughter when she was having a child." She glanced at Mary's face. "Let's make a meal, and we'll talk more when the men come in," she said.

They ate leisurely, avoiding the subject of the trip to Egypt until the meal was finished and the boys were put to bed for the night. "I have kept my curiosity to myself for as long as I can," Elizabeth finally exclaimed. "Tell us what has happened to you." So they told about the attitude of the townspeople, the trip to Bethlehem, the barn where Jesus was born. "Do you mean that you didn't even have a clean bed to rest in when you had the baby?" Elizabeth asked, aghast.

Mary's Story

"Your mother has much to answer for." But then they told about the angels, the shepherds, the Wise Men and their gifts, the angel's warning to Joseph that Herod was about to kill their child.

"You did hear about the death of 300 baby boys in Bethlehem, didn't you?" Joseph asked.

"We decided it was just another of Herod's senseless killings of Jews," Zacharias answered. "Do you mean to tell us that senseless destruction was aimed at destroying Jesus because the Wise Men called him the king of the Jews?"

"Exactly, which is why we went to Egypt," Mary continued the story. "An angel came to Joseph in a dream at night. Right after the Wise Men left, in fact. We packed up in the middle of the night and walked with the donkey to Hebron, where we traded the donkey for the horses. It took nearly two weeks to get to Succoth, and while we were there we heard about the babies killed in Bethlehem. After we heard about that, we went to Heliopolis." She went on to describe that Mecca for Jews in the middle of what used to be the country of their slavery.

"So we plan to return to Bethlehem," Mary's voice held a tinge of excitement.

"You shouldn't," Zacharias warned.

"We shouldn't? Herod is dead. The angel told me," Joseph replied.

"True." Zacharias scratched his beard thoughtfully. "But the Ethnarch of Judea is Archelaus. He began with fine words and promises, but when a group of Jewish leaders went to him and requested the remission of punishment for and the release of political prisoners, he refused."[1]

"He refused to lower taxes," Elizabeth took up. "We are paying as much, if not more, now."

Mary and Joseph looked at each other.

"He did worse than that," Zacharias went on. "When the people protested his high-handed treatment, his soldiers entered the temple court. They said they were there to keep order, but the people in the temple court naturally resisted them. Then Archelaus sent an even larger group of soldiers. Three thousand Jews were killed."

"To make matters even worse," Zacharias' voice took on a deep note of sadness, "in the melee, the new administrator of Syria, a man named Sabinus, took advantage of all the battle, sneaked into the temple treasury and robbed everything he and his men could carry out. The temple gold is gone."

Joseph and Mary gasped at this desecration of their holy temple. "Since you have been gone, you may not have heard that Herod became ill. It was after the massacre of the babies, I think," Elizabeth said pensively.

"Oh, yes," Zacharias again took up the story. "People were so angry with his treatment of Bethlehem and his heavy taxes, that when they found out he was sick, they had a celebration in the streets of Jerusalem. A mob tore down the golden eagle that he had placed over the gate of the temple."[2]

1　*The SDA Bible Commentary*, vol. 5, pp. 63, 64.
2　*The SDA Bible Commentary*, vol. 5, p. 42.

Going Home Again

"But then he died?" Joseph asked.

"Unfortunately, no," Zacharias replied. "He recovered. He ordered Salome—you know of his sister?" At Joseph's nod, he continued. "He ordered her to take all the leaders of the Jews and imprison them in the hippodrome. She did that. He ordered that upon his death all the imprisoned Jews be killed so people would mourn."

"And did she kill them?" Joseph wondered about those few leaders whom he knew.

"No, she let them go," Zacharias answered, "but many of them were in the revolt when Archelaus became Ethnarch, and he had them all killed, so we have lost many of our religious leaders anyway."

"What do you suggest we do?" Mary asked quietly.

Zacharias thought carefully before replying, then said slowly, "In spite of the treatment you received in Nazareth, that will be the safest place for you to live. Herod Antipas is the Tetrarch of Galilee and Paraea. People still don't like the taxes he charges, but he has been a much more moderate ruler than Archelaus. I wouldn't be surprised to see Archelaus lose his throne. I understand there is talk of sending a delegation of Jews to Rome soon to request his dethronement. But I still think you will be safer in Nazareth."

Joseph glanced at Mary. Remembering the townspeople's treatment of her before the birth of Jesus, he wondered about moving back there, but they still had the house. "We'll talk it over," he promised Zacharias.

Joseph and Mary talked quietly on their sleeping mats long into the night. That night Joseph had another dream. The angel told him to go to Nazareth.

In the morning they had decided. They agreed with Zacharias that Nazareth would indeed be the safest haven for Jesus. The fact that most of the successful rebels still lived in Galilee and had not been killed bode well for the safety of that area. Jerusalem, and places near it, such as Bethlehem, could not be considered safe.

Since it was so close to Sabbath, they stayed with their relatives a little longer, and on the next first day they began the journey north. It was not what Mary imagined when they were crossing the desert. She had never believed she would return to Nazareth.

VI

Nazareth

Chapter 17

North to Nazareth

As they traveled the road north toward Nazareth, Mary felt the light had gone out of her life. If it hadn't been for the demands Jesus made on her, she wouldn't have cared where and how they traveled. She wanted the trip to never end. She dreaded facing what they had left behind. There was a fall chill in the air, but she wished to camp out forever. Winter in the wilds could be no less punishing than the cold she would face again in Nazareth, she was sure.

Although she shared none of her thoughts with Joseph, he was aware of her change in mood. No longer did she laugh at Jesus' antics. She cared for him perfunctorily, handing him to Joseph when she finished. When they camped, she wandered away alone.

At the last camping place before they reached Nazareth, Joseph called a day's halt to the trip. He unloaded the packs and began to go through the clothes pack. Mary watched with disinterest. *It didn't much matter what he did*, she thought. At last Joseph pulled out the new clothes they had bought with the money from the Magi in Egypt. They were of fine fabric, wonderful colors, the best Mary and Joseph had ever owned. Joseph lay the clothes out on bushes to take the wrinkles from them.

He made camp carefully near the stream, under the trees, beyond the hill that separated the road from the stream. Mary realized with a start of surprise that this was the same place she had rested at with Cleophas and Mary as they traveled to Elizabeth's house. It seemed so long ago and so far away now. So much had happened to her since that time.

Joseph prepared meals and encouraged Mary to eat for the sake of the child. And she ate, for the sake of the child. That night when they lay on their sleeping mat, Joseph placed Jesus in front of Mary, pulled her against himself, and held her tightly. For the first time on this trip, Mary began to feel. Tears splashed on the baby's soft hair, slowly at first, then with more momentum as she sobbed. Joseph said nothing. Simply held her in his strong arms until the sobs subsided. At last he spoke.

"In the morning, we will wash in the stream," he said softly near her ear. "We will put on our best clothes and we will ride into Nazareth in style."

"Will that make any difference?"

"I'm not sure," Joseph replied slowly, "but you saw Zacharias' and Elizabeth's reaction to our newly acquired wealth. Unfortunately, money impresses people." He paused as if to gather his thoughts. "With four horses and our new clothes, people will be impressed. Impressed people act differently toward you than those who think you have nothing."

Mary sniffed away the last of her tears.

"We will ride into town as if we own the world," Joseph said quietly. "We will ignore the stares; we will act like the stiffest of the Pharisees. We will stare straight ahead and ride directly to our home. We will unpack while people are watching. We will leave some of the gift boxes of the Magi out where they will be noticed. We will do it all without talking to anyone. People will be curious. But we will not talk to anyone until we are settled. Then we will wait for them to come to us."

Mary heaved a great sigh of relief. "Do you think it will work?"

"We will wear our good clothes until we return to our normal routine. I will bring in the water and wood and oil. You will not leave the house." Joseph paused. "I will have to purchase food for the winter, since we were not here to raise a garden. Thank God for the gifts of the Magi."

Mary wrapped her arms around the baby. She turned to face Joseph with Jesus between them. Warmth flooded through her at the love and care Joseph had evidenced. No other man in the world would have been a better husband to her through all that she had been through. God may have done incomprehensible things by giving her Jesus, but He had blessed her abundantly with the husband He had chosen for her. Mary kissed Joseph's lips. "Thank you," she said.

Joseph held her close, and they slept then.

In the morning they did as Joseph had planned. Mary ate a hearty breakfast, took herself to the stream to wash, taking time to wash the dust, accumulated during their travels, from her hair as well as her body. Then she dressed carefully in the finest garments she owned. She took care of Jesus while Joseph washed and dressed, dressing the baby in fine clothes too. Carefully they packed away their dusty clothes. Joseph pulled the burnooses from the pack. He handed Mary hers and donned his.

"These will keep the dust from our clothes until we get near Nazareth," he said. "We will take them off just before we enter town."

As the sun climbed to its zenith, they rode ever closer to Nazareth. Nervous energy seemed to fill Mary. Would Joseph's plan work? They stopped when the sun reached the top of the sky to eat and remove their outer clothes. They hid the burnooses in the packs and carefully remounted. Slowly they walked the horses into the edge of Nazareth. Joseph had timed heir entry carefully. They had entered town when people were out on the streets before the noon meal, and before they stopped work for the day to rest in the heat. The streets were full.

They rode stiff as Pharisees through the center of the village. Mary looked neither to the right nor left, though she could feel the stares of the townspeople. She knew Joseph was doing the same. She rode to the front door of their house, where Joseph unnecessarily helped Mary from her horse, holding the baby while she adjusted her clothes. He unloaded some of the packs from one horse, opened them, and carelessly strewed the contents as if looking for something, letting the townspeople glimpse some of the glories of the Magi as he carried things into the house.

Mary stood watching for a short while, then turned, and with quiet dignity entered the house she thought she had left forever. Once she reached the sanctuary of her home, she stripped off her good clothes, dressed in an older garment, and grabbed a broom. The months had left dust on everything, and the mess they had made as they packed to leave was still as they had left it. There was much to do. Fortunately, Jesus napped, and as she worked making her house livable again, Mary's heart began to lighten. She began to hum, and then sing, full-throated psalms of King David. Joseph paused in his work to listen, then smiled. Mary could have done nothing better.

Although the curiosity of the townspeople had given way somewhat to their cravings for their noon meal, many forsook the luxury of their afternoon rest to watch, some openly, some surreptitiously, behind the windows of their homes. Joseph continued to slowly unpack the animals, curry them down, and lead them around to the stable.

As soon as that was done, he got water jugs and went to the well in the center of town to obtain water for the animals and for Mary to use in the house. He took stock of their larder, such as it was, and went out to purchase food and oil. He sensed the questions hanging in the air as he spent more money than a carpenter had a right to own. But no one questioned him out loud.

Mary had a simple meal ready and Jesus fed and changed when Joseph entered the house with his purchases. "Did you spend every last gerah we have?" Mary asked in surprise.

"Not quite," Joseph said ruefully, "but I certainly got their attention." He looked at Mary's clothes and her work-worn hands and said carefully, "Perhaps you had better clean up and change. We may have company yet before the day is finished." Mary considered the importance of his words, then slowly, nodding her head, went to do as he bid. She was thankful for his foresight when, just as they sat down to the meal and Joseph had said a prayer, a knock sounded at the door. Mary and Joseph exchanged glances. No one ever knocked on doors. Slowly Joseph rose to answer it.

As he pulled the door open, Mary glimpsed the man standing outside and stood slowly to her feet. "Shalom to you," the man greeted Joseph without a smile.

"Shalom to you," Joseph answered as solemnly. He stood back and gestured a welcome. Mary's father entered the house. Joseph looked outside to see who had come with him. He was alone. Joseph answered the unspoken question that hung between them. "As it was, it turned out to be the thing we were supposed to do. Jesus had to be born in Bethlehem."

"Nonsense," Heli sputtered. "What do you mean, *had* to be born in Bethlehem!" Heli paused and then said, "I am alone." Joseph closed the door.

Mary's Story

Mary tried to speak, cleared her throat, and then tried again. "Won't you join us for our meal, Father?" her voice sounded abnormal to her. She gestured to where she had been seated, and her father walked across the room to take her seat. As she went to get another dish, her father watched her without comment. She filled a pottery dish with fresh green vegetables topped with chopped olives, crushed almonds, olive oil, and lemon juice. She added a piece of fish and took it to her father.

"Thank you," he murmured, and as she went to sit away from the men, as was the custom, her father stopped her. "Join us here," he said. Mary glanced at Joseph, who nodded. She joined the men at the table. No one spoke for a moment. Mary took a bite of her food, but it tasted like straw. *What does my father want?* she wondered.

Finally, he spoke. "Why did you leave?"

"I was required to go to Bethlehem to be counted in the census," Joseph replied.

"But you shouldn't have taken Mary with you in her condition." Heli was more than a little upset, and it showed. "Where did she have the baby, in some common inn, without her mother or any woman to attend her?"

"Actually, no," Joseph replied. "She didn't have the baby in an inn."

Mary could stand it no longer. She spoke up. "Would my mother have attended me had I stayed here alone?" she asked quietly. "My mother disowned me; you wouldn't speak to me. The men in the village treated me like a ..." she choked. "The women wouldn't have anything to do with what they considered a loose woman. Who would have attended me?" Her voice became a little hysterical.

Joseph reached over and took her hand.

"I took Mary with me because I feared what might happen to her if I left her here."

"I didn't tell you," Mary spoke again, "who the messenger was who came to tell me of Elizabeth's pregnancy."

"No, I don't believe you did," Heli agreed.

"I didn't tell you the whole message he gave me either," Mary continued. "You see, it was difficult for me to believe, and I never thought he meant I would be pregnant right away."

"What are you saying?" her father exclaimed, jumping up from his chair. "Are you telling me that you were pregnant by a messenger, a person you had never seen before?"

"No." Mary realized what a muddle she was making of her explanation and looked to Joseph for help.

"If you will be seated again," Joseph said to Heli, "I think we can both explain to you what happened to Mary." Heli gave him a disbelieving look but returned to his seat. "The messenger who came to Mary was the same angel who spoke to Zacharias," Joseph said. "He also came to me when I had to make the decision whether or not to marry Mary."

Heli made as if to interrupt, but Joseph raised his hand to stop him and continued talking.

North to Nazareth

"The angel came to Mary and told her not to be afraid. He told her that God would give her a child in her womb, that he would be the Messiah. He told her to name the baby Jesus, for he would save his people from their sins. We don't understand that, but that is what the angel said. Then the angel told her about Elizabeth."

"When I got to Elizabeth's house, she knew already that I would be the mother of the Messiah," Mary continued the story. "What none of us knew then was that I was already pregnant. We think it was because the prophets said a virgin would conceive and have a child. I couldn't understand why God did it until I read that prophecy in the scrolls we bought in Egypt."

"In Egypt?" Heli sounded a bit faint.

Joseph began to talk again. "We left without telling you because we didn't think it would matter to you," he said. "Mary had the baby the night we arrived in Bethlehem. He was born in a stable, the only shelter we could find."

"A stable!" Heli exploded. "My grandson was born in a stable?"

"More than your grandson," Joseph said sternly. "He is not my son. He is the Son of God in heaven. If the stable was good enough for God, it should be good enough for your grandson."

Heli seemed to shrink into himself.

"The baby was barely born when the shepherds came," Mary said.

Heli shook his head as if to clear it.

Mary continued, "The shepherds said that angels had appeared to them where they were watching their sheep. They said that Jesus was born and he was wrapped in swaddling cloths and lying in a manger. They came to Bethlehem and found us. They worshiped the baby as the Son of God, and they told us the song the angels sang. A whole host of angels filled the heavens, they said, and they sang, 'Glory to God in the highest, and on earth peace, good will toward men.' The landlord's wife helped me to have the baby, and after the shepherds left, we slept a little. The shepherds stayed in the dining room of the inn, and the innkeeper's wife must not have slept at all the rest of the night, because the shepherds were there when we went in for breakfast."

"Everyone in the inn knew that Jesus was born to be king of the Jews," Joseph said, taking up the story. "They all came to see the baby, and one of the men gave us a house to live in. Then the Magi came."

"Magi?" Heli's voice sounded strangled.

"Wise Men from the East. They followed a star. We saw it right over our house. They came in the night, and at first we were frightened because we didn't know who they were and what they wanted, but the star was the most beautiful thing—the most glorious thing—I have ever seen. They told us they had followed the star for nearly a year and how it had brought them to our house. They came in and gave Jesus gifts of gold, frankincense, and myrrh. We have had enough to live on because of that."

"King Herod tried to kill Jesus," Mary said.

Mary's Story

"You know about the Slaughter of the Innocents in Bethlehem?" Joseph asked.

Heli nodded weakly.

Joseph continued to explain. "The Wise Men had gone to Jerusalem first. They tried to find out where we were by asking in the temple, and then Herod sent for them. He told them he wanted to worship Jesus too. But an angel came to them also. He said they were not to go back to Herod but leave another way and go home. They left as soon as they had seen Jesus. That morning before daylight, the angel—Gabriel again—came to me and told me we must go to Egypt immediately because Herod wanted to kill the baby."

"So we packed up and left before daylight," Mary said. "I don't know what the people in Bethlehem think of us."

"We walked to Hebron, where we bought the horses, and rode across the wilderness to Succoth. We arrived there and learned that Herod's men had killed 300 children in Bethlehem. That was also predicted in the Prophets: 'Thus saith the Lord; A voice was heard in Ramah, lamentation, and bitter weeping; Rachael weeping for her children refused to be comforted because they were not.'" Joseph quoted Jeremiah. "Because the angel told us to flee for Jesus' life, we knew Herod was trying to destroy our baby when he killed all those others."[1]

"I don't understand why he didn't warn the other mothers," Mary said quietly. "I can't stop hurting for them, for the loss of their babies."

"We went from Succoth to Heliopolis and were there about four months before the angel came to me again and told me that Herod was dead and we were to come back to Israel. We left immediately. We thought to settle back in Bethlehem, never to come back here again."

Heli made a sound between an exclamation and a sob, but Joseph continued. "We stopped to see Zacharias and Elizabeth," he said. "Zacharias said Jesus would be safer here. He says Archelaus is worse than Herod ever was. He has killed more people simply because they asked for leniency for political prisoners. And I had a dream that night. The angel appeared to me again. So we came back here. We didn't expect a welcome. We just want protection for Jesus."

Heli said not a word as he sat there. Odd emotions played across his face. Mary took another bite of her food. It tasted better.

Heli reached toward her. "Forgive me, Daughter," he said simply.

Tears started in Mary's eyes as she stared at her father. She placed her hand in his. "I forgive you. I probably would have acted worse than you have."

He had called her daughter. Never had a word sounded sweeter to Mary. Her father had taken her back again. She smiled mistily at him through her tears, then turned to smile at Joseph. He clasped her other hand. At that moment she felt she could never be happier.

"Oh, we didn't tell you about the prophets in the temple," she exclaimed. So they went on to tell about Simeon and Anna and how they prophesied that Jesus would be the king of Israel.

---

1   Matt. 2:17, 18

North to Nazareth

"Am I allowed to see this king?" Heli asked at length.

"Oh, yes," Mary said and then stood up quickly. Taking her father's hand, she led him to the next room, where Jesus lay asleep in his cradle. "There he is," she whispered.

Heli stood for a moment, looking down at the sleeping child. "He doesn't look much like a king," he said quietly. At last Heli drew a deep breath. "I must go. There is much to tell your mother. I hope …" he hesitated.

"That she will believe you?" Mary finished for him.

Heli gave her a twisted smile. "Something like that," he replied.

"Come and finish your food first," said Mary, smiling again.

Anna came the next morning. Her reaction to Jesus was as warm and as loving as Mary could have hoped. Heli had told her everything Mary and Joseph had told him. But she pressed for more details, which Mary supplied. And when she left, she hugged her daughter and apologized as her husband had apologized the night before.

Mary forgave her mother through her tears. She hadn't admitted to herself until now how much it meant to have her parents back again. Just before her mother left, Mary told her, "I am going to have another child. This will truly be my husband's firstborn, but I think Joseph will always treat Jesus as if he was his firstborn son."[2]

"I'm glad for you, Mary," Anna said. "You could not have found a better husband."

Mary's eyes twinkled. "I think so, too."

With her parents' acceptance, Mary noticed a gradual warming attitude by most of the townspeople, but there were some exceptions. The matchmaker was one. *The matchmaker never has approved of me, anyway,* Mary reasoned. *Life will go on without the world's approval.* She had learned that long ago.

---

[2] Four other sons of Mary and Joseph are named in the Bible: Joses, Simon, James, and Jude (or Judas). There are sisters mentioned also. Catholic tradition teaches that these children were from a previous marriage of Joseph's, but the Bible says that Joseph didn't know Mary until after Jesus was born. There is no evidence that the other children didn't belong to Mary. The reason for the Catholic tradition might be a reverence for Mary's supposed lifelong virginity.

Chapter 18

Passover Time

The winter passed and melted toward spring. One day Anna asked Mary if she and Joseph intended to attend Passover. Heli and Anna had always traveled to Jerusalem for the week-long festival. When her mother mentioned it to Mary, expecting her to be ready to go too, she put her mother off. Mary wanted to go. Not only would there be the religious ceremonies but she always met old friends she had made through the years of attending. But would it be safe?

She and Joseph talked it over that night. "Archelaus won't do anything during Passover," Joseph declared. "Besides, he thinks his father killed Jesus already."

So with uplifted heart, Mary prepared for the trip to Jerusalem, for the week that they would live in a tent attending Passover. Her second pregnancy was advancing, and Jesus had grown into an adventuresome little boy. He walked. He was curious about everything. He wasn't an exceptionally beautiful child, but his sunny disposition made him extraordinarily lovable. Everyone who came near him immediately took a liking to the little boy.

One day Mary took Jesus to visit Cleophas and Mary. She hadn't seen them since she left Cleophas with the soldiers. She hoped they would forgive her for abandoning him, but she felt she had no other choice. She couldn't expect Mary to come to her. Her ordeal with the robbers had left her ill, and Cleophas had never completely healed properly from his broken legs. She wanted to know that they forgave her before she went to Passover. As she hoped, they fell in love with Jesus.

"It wasn't your fault," Cleophas' wife, Mary, told her quietly when Joseph's Mary voiced her feelings. "You did what you had to do." She paused a moment. "Tell me about the angel. Your mother told me a little of your story." So Mary repeated the tale of the angel who had gone first to Zacharias, then to her, then to Joseph. She told again of the stable, the Wise Men, the flight to Egypt, the way the angel kept appearing to Joseph to protect Jesus from Herod.

"And you think it is safe to take Jesus to Jerusalem now?" Cleophas asked.

"If it is not," Mary replied with sincere faith, "then the angel will tell us." Passover was the highlight of the year. Of the three festivals required, it was the one everyone attended. Women weren't required to attend, but Mary had never missed going. She loved the ritual of searching out any leaven in the house, the fast before the feast, the ceremonial slaying of the lamb on the

Passover Time

fourteenth day, the feast of the Passover. She loved the story of how God had freed His people 1,000 years earlier from slavery to the Egyptians. She knew the story of Moses and the burning bush, of Aaron and his rod that budded, of the tabernacle built in the wilderness.[1] This year the story seemed more real to her because she had traveled the same desert. She wanted Jesus and the new baby she carried to have the same love for the religious rituals that she had.

Mary made herself a promise that she would teach her children to love her God as she did. This Passover trip was the continuation of her religious life. *I will never give up Passover as many other women have*, she told herself. *How can I teach my children to revere their heritage if I keep then away from the important religious festivals. I have seen it happen to others. The rites have become nothing more than a traditional thing to do.* Sadly, to most people who participated, the rites had nothing to do with God and one's devotion to Him.

So Mary attended Passover with her parents, Joseph, and their children—that year and every year thereafter. And at every other Passover, she added another child to the family. First Joses, born two years after Jesus, then Simon two years later. After the boys came her girls: Anna, named after her mother, and Elizabeth, after her cousin in the hill country. Then two more boys a little closer together. They made a great procession going to the Passover the year Jesus turned twelve. It was time for Jesus to be admitted to the Jewish manhood, the year for his Bar-Mitzvah.

Sometimes Mary had regretted the impossibility that Jesus could not attend the temple school. She taught her children long and well to be sure they learned about their heritage and understood the prophecies about the Messiah. Jesus showed special interest in those prophecies, understanding that they pointed to him. While Mary repeatedly pointed out the parts that showed he would be king and judge, he turned to the prophet Isaiah and read, "He is despised and rejected of men; a man of sorrows, and acquainted with grief; and we hid as it were our faces from him; he was despised, and we esteemed him not."[2]

"What does that mean?" the young Jesus would ask his mother, and she had to admit she didn't understand. When Mary couldn't answer Jesus' questions to his satisfaction, he took himself out in the hills, where he communed with God, where he learned what his earthly parents could not teach him.

The other children were satisfied to learn only what they must, to work in the carpentry shop with Joseph, while Jesus dug deeper, tried harder, and perfected everything he did. More and more often, he would take time from his day to visit the hills and talk with God.

Mary had no idea how much Jesus had learned until that Passover. As usual, they had made the trip to Jerusalem. They had gone through the rituals and rites of the service. The lamb was killed by the priest. Jesus went along, but this year he saw the slain lamb as a symbol of himself

---

1 Exod. 3:2–5; Num. 17:8
2 Isa. 53:3

Mary's Story

and tried to explain it to his parents. But Mary and Joseph didn't understand. They knew the prophecies of the Messiah. He would deliver his people from Roman rule. They didn't see any prophecies telling them the Messiah would be killed.

Dissatisfied with the shallow thinking of his parents and siblings, Jesus decided to seek out the school run by the rabbis during the Passover. Perhaps there he could get some answers to his questions.

On the last day, Jesus joined his parents for the feast before disappearing from the family. Mary was used to it. Jesus went off by himself so often that she no longer worried about him. Nothing had happened to him in twelve years of Passover festivals. Archelaus had died long ago. There seemed to be no reason to worry about Jesus. Besides, she was busy with the younger children. The babies needed to be put to bed and the older ones needed baths and evening lessons. The Passover rituals, while special to Mary, became more exhausting as time went on. This year she was ready to go home.

They left early the next morning. They had a donkey again for the little ones to ride. People thronged the roads out of Jerusalem—carts, animals, children. It was a good time to visit with friends as they began the journey. Those who lived closer would drop out, making plans to join them next year, while those who lived at the far reaches of the kingdom traveled on.

There was still a large crowd when they camped for the night. Wearily Mary put the little ones to bed, then looked around for Jesus. Usually he came to help her, but she hadn't seen him all day.

Still not greatly worried, she looked for Joseph. He and Heli were talking near the campfire.

"Have you seen Jesus?" she asked.

"I thought he was with you," Joseph replied.

"I haven't seen him all day." A little fear flickered. "I thought he might be with the other boys, but they don't know where he is either."

"I haven't seen him today either," Heli said. "What about your mother? Other relatives? Friends?"[3]

Joseph stood up. "You go see your mother, Mary. Heli can you check with the other relatives. I'll check the other campfires." Joseph strode off.

Heli patted Mary's arm comfortingly. "Go to your mother, then come back here," he said. "I'm sure we'll find him."

But they couldn't find him—an hour later they hadn't found him, two hours later they still hadn't found him, and Mary remembered the trip to Egypt. What if someone still wanted to kill her boy? Where could he be? By now everyone in the camp was looking for Jesus, but he seemed nowhere to be found. Mary became nearly frantic with worry.

"Leave the younger children with me," Anna said. "We'll wait here for you. You and Joseph

---

3 Luke 2:43–49 tells the story of Jesus being in the temple. Joseph and Mary searched for him.

Passover Time

go back to Jerusalem and look for him."

It was the middle of the night and very dark, but Mary was so worried she felt she could walk back to Jerusalem without sleeping or eating. She sure couldn't sleep without her boy, or eat, for that matter. So she and Joseph started to walk.

"Do you suppose he's dead?" Mary voiced her worst fear.

Joseph wrapped his arm around her shoulders. "I don't think so. Someone would have told us." He sounded only half-convinced, and his doubt lent wings to Mary's feet. The sun was coming up when they saw the outskirts of town.

"Oh, God, forgive me," Mary prayed. "You entrusted me with the care of this special boy, and I have been careless. Please help us find him. Please keep him safe."

They went immediately to the house of the friend in whose yard they had camped. "Shalom the house," Joseph shouted while he pounded on the door. He woke up the household.

"Shalom. Why, friends!" Nahum answered the door, sleepily. "I expected you to be halfway home by now."

Joseph's voice was rough. He didn't answer Nahum. He simply questioned, "Is Jesus here with you?"

"No. Isn't he with you?"

"I haven't seen him since the Passover feast," Mary replied. "Have you seen him at all?"

"Come to think if it, I don't think so," Nahum said, running his hands through his unruly hair. "Come on in, and I'll see what Martha knows."

But Martha knew as little as Mary and Joseph did. "Let me make you some food, though," she suggested.

"I don't have time!" Mary protested, frantic with worry. Fear gnawed at her insides and twisted her heart. "A sword shall pierce your own heart also," the old prophet Simeon had said. *This is what it must feel like*, she thought, twisting her hands together unconsciously.

Martha grasped her fluttering hands. "You have to keep up your strength. You've been walking all day and all night. Come eat something. Then we will help." So Mary tried to eat, though worry gnawed at her insides and nearly gagged her. *Where is Jesus? Is he hungry? Is he hurt? Is he alive?*

"We need to be organized about this," Nahum said when the meal was finished. "We need to divide the city into sectors and go house to house. With all of us working, we should be able to cover the homes at least." So they divided up the city. Nahum's and Martha's oldest children went two by two to homes nearest their own. Mary, Joseph, Nahum, and Martha each took a section of their own.

They returned that night weary, their search fruitless. Mary couldn't eat. They lay down to rest. Mary slept hard for two or three hours, then awoke to listen to the sounds of the night. "Forgive me, Lord," she prayed. "I am so sorry I didn't take better care of your Son. Please show

Mary's Story

me where he is." But her prayers seemed unanswered.

They searched all the next day. Joseph was as worried as Mary was now. *Perhaps there is some foul play,* she thought. That night they lay together on their sleeping mat, clinging to each other for strength. "God will take care of him," Joseph tried to assure Mary.

"He used us to take care of him before," Mary reminded Joseph. "We neglected him when we should have been watching him. We have grown careless. He has so many enemies. What if— "

"Sh-h-h-h." Joseph held her close and comforted her. "The angel would have warned us if there was any real danger. You know that he always has before."

"We haven't seen the angel for a very long time. Do you suppose God has forgotten about Jesus? He isn't answering my prayers."

"No, I don't think so," Joseph said. But to Mary's ears Joseph didn't sound completely convinced. The next morning they began again, going from house to house. That evening they had covered the town. The whole city had a description of Jesus, knew that he was missing, but no one came forward with an answer.

Martha was the last one in. "I talked to the wife of one of the rabbis today," she said. "She thought it a little strange that her husband hasn't been home for several days. But then she said that he is probably cleaning up the temple after Passover. It may have been more work than he expected."

Mary was so tired and worried that she nodded at Martha's words and went to lie down on her sleeping mat. Nothing mattered. Her other children, her parents, even Joseph. If she lost Jesus, she didn't think her life could be worth living.

It wasn't long before Joseph joined her again. "There's only one place in town that he might be that we haven't looked," he said.

"Where?" a little bit of hope filled Mary's heart.

"The temple."

"Why would he be there?" Mary wondered aloud.

"He's always asking questions."

Mary didn't make the connection.

When she didn't answer, Joseph continued, "Maybe he's talking to the rabbis."

"Of course, why didn't we think of that first?" Mary sat up abruptly. "Let's go and see."

But Joseph pulled her back down on the mat. "They'll all be asleep by now. We'll go first thing in the morning." Mary spent another sleepless night. This time she dared hope, though. Despair lurked in the corners, but hope made a bright spot in the middle of her mind. Maybe she would find her boy yet.

The next morning they hurried to the temple. Through the court of the Gentiles and the court of the women they crossed to the schoolroom. Voices echoed in the now empty halls, and

Passover Time

Rabbis spoke one at a time, telling the prophecies of the Messiah. Mary knew them all by heart.

"The Messiah will not come before the messenger comes," one priest spoke. "Isaiah has prophesied in the writings of Malachi: 'Behold I will send my messenger, and he shall prepare the way before me; he will come in the power and the spirit of Elijah.'[4] We haven't seen that messenger yet. Isaiah says 'he will come to his temple, even the messenger of the covenant.'"

And then they heard Jesus' voice. "Will you explain to me what Malachi means, then, when he says in the same place 'and the Lord, whom ye seek, shall suddenly come to his temple,'[5] and doesn't it equate the Lord whom you seek with the messenger in that verse?"

"I never thought of it that way before," the rabbi replied slowly.

Jesus pressed on. "And what about the next part? What does it mean where it says no one will abide the day of his coming?"[6]

"Why, of course that is talking of the enemies of our kingdom," another rabbi spoke up. "Then why does Isaiah say he will 'purify the sons of Levi and purge them as gold and silver, that they may offer unto the Lord an offering in righteousness?'"[7]

"Why, you know, son, that is why we wear the phylacteries, why we do good works, to give the Lord an offering of our righteousness," was the response.

"But aren't you aware that Isaiah also said your righteousness is filthy rags?"[8] Jesus asked. Then he paused. No one answered him. "Perhaps there is more to the Messiah than we think," he continued. "There are other verses that describe the Messiah as a shepherd, as a physician, as a suffering sacrifice. The temple services, the slain lamb, all point to the Messiah. Don't you recall when the first parents sinned in the garden? The lamb pointed to the Messiah, who would be slain for their sins."

"How did you come to have such insights into the Scriptures?" asked one of the priests. "You weren't taught here. Did you attend the temple school in Heliopolis?"

"No, I did not" Jesus answered. "I have spent most of my life since I was a little baby in Nazareth."

It was enough for Mary. She barged into the classroom, Joseph right behind her. She didn't know or care if he was there to support her or stop her. "Jesus, son, why have you done this? Why didn't you come home with us? Do you know how long we have been searching for you? We were worried sick that something terrible had happened to you."

Jesus looked at his mother's face—torn with anguish, fear, anger—and he understood. "Why did you look for me?" he asked innocently. "You knew that I had to be about my Father's business."[9]

---

4   Mal. 3:1
5   Mal. 3:2
6   Ibid.
7   Mal. 3:3
8   Isa. 64:6
9   Luke 2:49

Mary's Story

"Your father's business needs your hands right now," Joseph spoke up sternly, "We have more work in our business than I can handle, and the boys aren't able to do what you can do. Come. Let's go home."

Mary, thankful that Jesus was safe, let her fears turn to anger. "You have caused enough trouble and wasted enough of the rabbi's time. The rest of the family has gone on, I hope. Your grandmother is caring for the younger children. You have given us grief for three days. Come."

So Jesus went. There wouldn't be any more talks with the rabbis that day. Maybe not until next year, he realized.

VII
His Father's Business

Chapter 19

Baptism

As the years passed, Jesus continued to work with Joseph, study the Scriptures and other writings Joseph had bought in Egypt, and commune with God by disappearing into the hills. Mary didn't mind his going out into the hills because he always did his work first. In fact, Jesus gave her far less problems than her other children did. But because she didn't have to concern herself much with Jesus as he matured, everyday occupations and challenges with her other children and with work made it easy to forget that Jesus was someone special.

Gradually, the people in the village accepted Jesus and accepted Mary, her life, her faithfulness to her family. Jesus' personality won them over. In fact, they forgot their charge that he was illegitimate and called him Joseph's son. Even Cleophas, Joseph's brother, seemed to soften toward Mary. His wife, Mary, who still suffered from her ordeal with the robbers, seemed to blame Mary somehow for her illness. It became obvious to both Mary and Joseph that most of the people in the village of Nazareth didn't understand and probably never would. They loved the boy, but they didn't accept the story of the angels or that he was the Messiah.

As the children grew, Jesus spent less time in the carpentry shop, turning more and more of the work over to Jonas and Simon. Jesus also talked to his brothers, trying to explain to them what he had learned from the Torah. James and Jude seemed more interested in what Jesus said than their older brothers were.

Joseph grew more stooped with the years. Old injuries began to pain him more as the days went by. One day he turned the business over to the younger generation and spent more time in the sun. He said it made him ache less.

Heli died, then Anna. Joseph talked more to Cleophas. Gradually, Cleophas began to understand a little more of the story, to accept the idea that Jesus would be the king of Israel one day, and to accept that perhaps Jesus truly was special, because of the way Jesus himself behaved.

One day when Mary awoke, Joseph, who was beside her, was uncommonly quiet. She realized that sometime in the night, he had slipped quietly into eternal sleep. Grief filled her being. How would she get along without him? How would they all survive without Joseph? She began wailing, and her children all gathered around her. Jesus, Jonas, Simon, James, Anna, Elizabeth, and Jude. She felt proud of her children, all grown so strong. Her baby was nearly eighteen years old. Jesus, nearly thirty, still had that kindness about him that set him apart and made everyone love him. They laid Joseph to rest in a tomb near Nazareth, and life went on, though Mary grieved.

Shortly after that, however, things started to change. Someone brought a message to town that a prophet like Elijah was preaching and baptizing at the Jordan. He was dressed, they said, in camel skins with a leather belt. He claimed he ate wild locusts and honey, they said. He seemed healthy, though, and his message was interesting. He denounced sin wherever he saw it, even denouncing Herod for his lifestyle.

Herod Antipas had taken his brother Phillip's wife, Herodias, as his own wife. She and her daughter, Salome, and Salome's husband, the other Phillip, lived in the palace with Antipas. This prophet had the temerity to condemn their lifestyle, the sins of the leaders of Israel, and the sins of the common people. He called on everyone to repent, and he was baptizing people in the muddy waters of the Jordan.

Herod Antipas sent soldiers for riot control; the chief priest sent representatives to ascertain this prophet's message; zealots joined the crowd looking for the real Messiah; the curious came as they always did, for relief from boredom. A few, on the other hand, came because they really believed what the prophet was saying; some were converted and baptized.

"I am going to the Jordan," Jesus announced one day.

"You aren't going alone," Mary declared. "I think this is Elizabeth's son, and I want to hear what he is saying."

So the family traveled down the Jordan to see who this was. Mary knew, of course, as soon as she heard John's voice. "Repent, and be baptized every one of you," his voice boomed through the valley. He sounded exactly like his father, Zacharias.

"John," she whispered. All those years ago when Elizabeth had welcomed her with the message that the baby in her bosom knew who the mother of the Lord was, Mary had wondered about John.

"Repent ye; for the kingdom of heaven is at hand. For I am he that was spoken of by the prophet Isaiah, saying, 'the voice of one crying in the wilderness, "Prepare the way of the Lord, make his paths straight."'"[1]

Mary looked at him. Tall, broad-shouldered, he was dressed in an odd-looking garment woven from camel's hair, and he wore a wide leather belt around his waist. He was good-looking, but people were mainly interested in his message. They flocked in groups to be baptized, and he baptized them even while he continued to call others to follow. She was moved to be baptized herself.

Even some Pharisees and Sadducees came to be baptized, but when John saw them, he was outraged.

---

[1] Mark 1:3

Baptism

"O generation of vipers!" he called them. Mary was shocked at his words, even though they had heard rumors of his outspoken comments when it came to sin. "Who hath warned you to flee from the wrath to come? Bring forth fruits meet for repentance: and think not to say within yourselves, 'We have Abraham to our father;' for I say unto you, that God is able of these stones to raise up children unto Abraham."[2] There was total silence in the crowd. The only sound was the wind sighing through the Pampas Grass that edged the river. Mary, along with the others there, waited with baited breath to see the Pharisees' and Sadducees' reaction. The one thing they had in common was their pride in their national heritage and their demand for respect and honor.

"And now also the axe is laid unto the root of the trees: every tree therefore which bringeth not forth good fruit is hewn down and cast into the fire,"[3] John proclaimed. Some of the Pharisees turned away. Some of the Sadducees conferred with one another. Some of them stepped into the river in spite of John's harsh words and were baptized. People shuffled their feet.

"What shall we do to show these good fruits you speak of?" a man asked.

"He that hath two coats, let him impart to him that hath none," John replied. "And he that hath meat, let him do likewise."[4] Only the rich among them had more than one coat. Few of the poorer people had more than enough food to remain intact and alive each day. People looked at the Pharisees and Sadducees. What would they say?

But a publican, or tax collector, in the crowd spoke up. "That's well and good for them, but what shall we do?"

"Exact no more than that which is appointed to you," John replied.[5] The crowd laughed.

Everyone knew the publicans collected whatever the common man would bear. Part of his collection was indeed honest taxes, if there was such a thing as an "honest" tax. The remainder he would keep for himself.

One of the Roman guards stepped up. "What is required of us?" he asked.

"Do violence to no man, neither accuse any falsely; and be content with your wages," John replied.[6]

Murmurs ran through the crowd. No one had ever spoken like this to anyone before. This man was so different. Could this be the Messiah they were waiting for? Their murmurs increased in volume until John shouted to be heard above them.

"With water I baptize those who repent of their sins; but someone else is coming, someone greater than I am, so great that I am not worthy to carry his shoes! He shall baptize you with the Holy Spirit and with fire. He will separate the chaff from the grain, burning the chaff with

---

2   Luke 3:8
3   Matt. 3:10
4   Luke 3:11
5   Luke 3:13
6   Luke 3:14

Mary's Story

unquenchable fire, and storing away the grain."[7]

Mary felt Jesus move beside her and watched as he made his way through the crowd to John. "Baptize me," he said quietly.

"You should baptize me," John replied in humility and astonishment. "I'm not going to baptize you; why have you come to me?"

"Suffer it now to be so, for thus it becometh us to fulfill all righteousness," Jesus answered.[8]

Without further argument, John led Jesus into the water. A priest near Mary muttered. "That's the illegitimate Samaritan his mother is trying to pass off as a descendant of Father Abraham." He didn't bother to keep his voice pitched so his companion only could hear him. Mary wondered, *Why did he call Jesus a Samaritan?*

"This is the man whose mother was a prostitute?" another priest asked. "You mean he has the temerity to think he is something special?"

"Oh, yes," the first priest answered. "They brought him to the temple as a baby, claiming he was the son of her husband. Thank God I knew better. You can be sure I didn't record his name in the genealogy as a child of Abraham."

The chill Mary felt settled in a cold dread around her heart. *What, exactly, had the priest written in the genealogy?* As she thought about it, she remembered that neither she nor Joseph had seen the record. At Passover one of the boys must get a look at that book. If the name was wrong, it must be changed!

John and Jesus came out of the water, dripping. Jesus knelt on the bank of the river. A flash of light made the bright day brighter still. Thunder rumbled in a cloudless sky. A bird winged its way to light on Jesus' head. Mary understood the voice. "This is my beloved Son, in whom I am well pleased. Hear ye him."[9]

She glanced again at the priest, knowing that if he heard the voice, he would at last understand, but the look on the priest's face hadn't changed, except that he looked a little puzzled.

"Did you hear the voice?" someone asked.

"What voice," the priest jeered. "Thunder and lightning, and you hear a voice?"

"And see a bird," someone else remarked, "on top of his head."

"You're seeing things," the priest scoffed. "You're hallucinating."

Mary edged through the crowd away from the priests. Suddenly, Jesus stood beside her. "I must leave," he said. "This time, Mother, my Father has really called me to do His work."

Mary looked at him wordlessly for a long moment. She saw determination and a new sadness in his face. She nodded. The time indeed had come. She stood and watched while he walked away into the wilderness. He would learn some way from his Father how to be king of Israel.

---

7   See Matt. 3:11, 12
8   Matt. 3:13–15
9   See Matt. 3:16, 17

Chapter 20

The Wedding

The gossip grapevine was working well, Mary noted, as she prepared for Elizabeth's wedding. Jonas had followed Jesus to the edge of the wilderness, and they had not heard from or about him for over a month. Mary knew he would be talking with God during that time. It was the thing Jesus had done more and more often. When rumors began that Jesus had appeared again near the Sea of Galilee, Jonas had gone to check it out. He came back reporting that Jesus was gathering a band of followers: fishermen, a tax collector, and Jude and James. *At least he chose his brothers,* Mary thought.

Rumors circulated that one of his followers, a fisherman named Peter, was a man given to rushing in where angels feared to tread. Two other men he had especially called were other fishermen, James and John, the sons of Zebedee. Their nickname, because of their uncontrollable tempers, was the "Sons of Thunder." Mary wondered at Jesus' choices.

Why is he surrounding himself with uneducated fishermen? She wondered how differently things would have turned out if they had moved back to Bethlehem, nearer Jerusalem, where Jesus would have had access to the schools of the rabbis and had made friends with people in a position to help him in his quest to be king. *For a future king of Israel, he really is not doing the right things*, thought Mary. She fretted, stewed, worried. But Jesus kept doing what he wanted to do, and nothing anyone said to him dissuaded him from his decisions.

She had hoped when he returned from his communion in the wilderness that he would travel to Jerusalem, announce his coronation, and take over the country as king, banishing the Roman rulers to their foreign soil, where they belonged. She had been proud of his decision to begin his rule of his country. At thirteen in the temple, he was too young to understand the momentous calling he had. At thirty, he should certainly understand the importance of his kingship. Instead he spent his time by the Lake of Gennesaret, which some locals incorrectly called a sea.

Mary sighed as she added the last touches to Elizabeth's wedding dress. Jesus and his followers had all been invited to the wedding because Jesus wouldn't go anywhere without the men he had chosen to work with him. She just hoped they would mind their manners and know how to behave politely in common society. She would hate to have Elizabeth's wedding spoiled by a fight between those two hot-heads Jesus had insisted on calling to his side.

Mary's Story

However, Mary was surprised when she finally met the men. *Maybe Jesus' influence has indeed softened them,* she thought. *Or maybe the stories were exaggerated,* she admitted, remembering the rumors and downright lies that ruined her own reputation. She was especially pleasantly surprised by Judas Iscariot. Cultured and obviously well-taught and well-connected, he was exactly the kind of person she expected Jesus to connect with.

The wedding went well. The feasting and dancing lasted from dawn until long after dark each day. Mary threw herself into making her daughter's wedding memorable, making it what her own wedding should have been. The third day they ran out of wine. She immediately went in search of her son.

"Jesus," she said when she found him, "they have no wine."

"That's not my problem," Jesus answered. "My time has not yet come."

Ignoring her son's protest, Mary turned to the servants. "Whatever he tells you to do, do it," she said earnestly with complete faith that Jesus would not let her or his sister down.

Sitting in the doorway were the large water pots used to store the household water. Most of the water was gone because of the coming and going of many guests. Everyone who came had their feet washed by a servant, several of whom stood by waiting for another guest to arrive. Looking at the servants, Jesus said, "Fill the water pots full."

One of the men looked at Mary as if to protest. "Do as he says," she repeated to him.

It took time to fill the pots—six of them—each holding thirty gallons of water. The men made several trips to the well in the center of town but Jesus wasn't satisfied until each pot was brimming full to the top. When he was satisfied they couldn't put another drop in any of the jars, he said, "Take a cup, fill it with the water, and take it to the governor of the feast."

The servants looked at one another. The man was obviously demented. He expected to pass off water as wine? But they did what they were told. The governor took one sip of the water and demanded, "Where is your master?"

One of the servants stepped timidly forward. "I'll take you to him, sir."

The others followed behind, wondering what the bridegroom would say when he learned they were trying to pass plain well water as wine. And what would happen to them? The governor stopped in front of the groom. "What is the meaning of this?" he demanded. The servants shook.

"Of what?" the bridegroom asked.

"Every man for whom I have governed the wedding feast has set out his best wine at the beginning of the feast," the governor stated, "but not you. You first set out the wine of lowest quality, which wasn't too bad," he conceded, "and saved the best for last."

"I don't know what you're talking about," Elizabeth's new husband told the governor. Passing him the cup, the governor told him to taste it. Shock registered on the bridegroom's face as he tasted the water made into wine, "Where did this come from?" he demanded of the servants. "I have never tasted wine so good!"

The Wedding

"Jesus made it," one of the servants replied, "from well water."[1]

Elizabeth's new husband looked at his bride with new respect. "I see I have acquired not only a beautiful bride but a very resourceful brother-in-law," he said.

---

[1] The story of Jesus' first miracle is found in John 2:1–11.

Chapter 21

Born Again

The rest of the wedding week passed quickly. Jesus, along with his brothers, took Elizabeth to her bridegroom's bed chamber the last night of the wedding. His part of the ceremony was over. He heaved a sigh of relief. The last of his two sisters was safely married, and he could carry on his work now without so many family obligations. As soon as the wedding was officially over, Andrew invited Jesus, his mother, brother, and the rest of the disciples to his house. There, in Capernaum, at the edge of the Sea of Galilee, they spent an idyllic few days of vacation.

Mary had to admit when she saw the lake again that it was almost large enough to be called a sea. Andrew told her it was seven and a half miles across the lake and twelve and a half miles end to end. He and his brother, Peter—the impetuous disciple of Jesus—had fished every mile of it, he told Mary proudly. It was big enough to cause a boat plenty of trouble in a storm, he assured her.

While she enjoyed the sea, the coolness, the rest after the wedding preparations, and the work of the week-long wedding itself, Mary wanted to make the trip to Jerusalem for the Passover. She had missed very few Passovers, and she didn't want to do so now, even for the pleasures of a seaside vacation. So they all traveled the familiar road to Jerusalem. Jesus, Peter, Andrew, James and John—the Sons of Thunder, who mercifully kept the disagreements to a minimum—Judas Iscariot, Joses, Simon, Jude, and James, her younger sons. On the way her daughters and their husbands joined the procession, the new bridegroom taking his fair share of teasing and Elizabeth blushing at her brothers' remarks.

With such a large group traveling together, the trip seemed short, and soon they reached Jerusalem. It was nearly the time of the evening sacrifice when they entered the city, and Mary wanted to go to the evening service, so Jesus agreed to accompany her. Although he had missed Passover as a baby, Jesus couldn't remember not being at one, but he seemed to see it all this year with new eyes. He brooded over the market stalls, the cattle and sheep pens, the dove cages. And when they returned to their place of abode, he found some cords and knotted them into a scourge. Although Mary tried to get him to explain himself, he simply seemed more locked into his strange new disposition, and he sat for the rest of the evening, slapping the whip he had created against the palm of his hand.

Born Again

In the morning, they all went to the temple again. Mary planned to worship as always in the court of the women, but they had no more than entered the outer court when Jesus raised the whip he carried in his hand and marched over to the money-changers' table, thrusting aside the crowd as he went. Jesus dumped out the money and turned over the table. His demeanor was such that no one questioned his authority. He systematically went around the outer court, dumping money, overturning tables, opening cages and pens. As he went he repeated over and over, "Take these things hence! Make not my Father's house a house of merchandise."[1] The small whip of cords in his hand stunned the men whom he threatened. To the last man, they deserted the outer court. He repeated his mission in the inner courts of the temple. Mary watched as the men came running out. Peter later told her what happened.

"What reason do you have to do this?" a priest asked him. "By what sign will you show us that you have the authority to do this?"

"Destroy this temple and in three days I will raise it up."

"Three days," scoffed the priest. "This temple was built by many men working forty-six years, and you will build it in three days?" he mocked.

Mary didn't understand him any more than the priests did. What did Jesus mean? Build it in three days? Oh, well, she would just have to leave it up to God. God would teach him. He would learn somehow from his Father how to be king of Israel.

Uppermost in her mind since John's baptism of Jesus was the priest's remark that Jesus was a Samaritan. Samaritans, Mary knew, were considered the lowest of the low; the dogs that roamed the streets of any town were considered better than them. To call her baby, the Son of God, a Samaritan, well— "See what Jesus' name is in the genealogy," she requested of Joses.

Joses gave her a strange look. He hadn't heard the priest's remarks, so he had no idea why his mother would want to know this after all these years. Jesus ben Joseph, just like his name was Joses ben Joseph, he would wager. His surprise at the discovery of his older bother's recorded name still showed on his face as he shared the information with his mother. "Jesus ben Panthera, Jesus ibn Maryum."

Mary's face went white, and she reeled. Joses caught her. "Mother?"

"That's why the priest of Nazareth keeps calling Jesus a Samaritan," Mary murmured. "He's the one who entered the name in the books. I wonder how he came to that conclusion?" Her mind strayed to the handsome soldier who had helped her so many years before, and she gasped. "I wonder how he knew about Panthera."

"Who is Panthera? You always told me Jesus was special. You said he was the Son of God. You never said anything about a Panthera."

And then, of course she had to explain her remarks. "But I don't understand the genealogical entry," she said to Joses. "I hadn't seen that soldier for months …" her voice trailed off. "On

---

1 This cleansing of the temple is found in John 2:13–20.

Mary's Story

the trip, of course," she said as if to herself. "He must have seen me after Mary was taken and Cleophas hurt." She told Joses the rest of the story.

Jesus spent the next few days healing people; anyone who was sick he would heal simply by a touch or by a word or two. Many people believed he was someone special when he performed miracles, and Mary began to wonder what other surprises he had in store.

Late one night she found out. She was disturbed by voices under her window. It was Jesus and, from the sound if it, one of the rabbis. Curious, she stole to the window to see what was happening so late. Jesus stood in the shadows under a tall sycamore tree; another man, dressed, she could tell, in the robes of a Pharisee, stood close to him. Although their voices were quite low, they carried plainly to her. She turned away to go back to her sleeping mat, when Jesus' voice stopped her.

"Except a man be born of water and the spirit, he cannot see the kingdom of God," Jesus said.

"How can a man be born when he is old?" the Pharisee questioned.

Mary concurred in her mind with the Pharisee's question. The ambiguous statement about birth and rebirth made her wonder, as she often had in the past, about the miracle of her co-operation with the Holy Spirit to bring Jesus into the world. Even though she experienced the miracle, she could not begin to grasp how God had done it; all she could do was trust. And now, with Nicodemus' question, Mary was led to contemplate what Jesus could possibly have meant when he said that one must be "born of water and the spirit."

"Except a man be born of water and the spirit, he cannot see the kingdom of God."

Mary drew a deep breath and held it as Jesus continued. "That which is born of the flesh is flesh; and that which is born of the Spirit is spirit. You shouldn't be surprised that I said you must be born again. Look at the wind. It blows where it will, and you hear the sound of it, but you can't see where it comes form or where it goes. So is everyone who is born of the spirit."

"How can these things be?" the Pharisee asked.

"Aren't you a teacher in Israel, and you don't understand these things?" Jesus replied. "If you can't understand the simple things of earth, how do you expect to understand the complex things of heaven?"

When the Pharisee didn't answer, Jesus continued, "As Moses lifted up the serpent in the wilderness, even so must the Son of man be lifted up that whosoever believeth in him should not perish but have everlasting life. For God so loved the world that He gave His only begotten Son that whosoever believeth in him should not perish but have everlasting life. For God sent not his Son into the world to condemn the world but that the world through him might be saved.

"He who believes in him is not condemned; but he who does not believe is condemned already because he has not believed in the name of the only begotten Son of God."[2]

---
2   Jesus' conversation with Nicodemus is found in John 3:1–21.

Born Again

Although Jesus continued to talk to the Pharisee, Mary slipped back to her mat. She had heard enough to keep her awake for a long time. As she lay there, she reviewed the things the angel told her when she first learned that Jesus would be her son, the safety God had provided for Jesus, the time when the angel came to Joseph by night to warn him of Herod's schemes. She thought about how different Jesus had always been from his brothers and sisters.

Now she heard Jesus say he must be lifted up on a stake like the serpent in the wilderness. Surely he didn't really mean that. He would be lifted up on a throne and all men would be drawn to him as king of Israel. That must be his meaning. Comforted by her reasoning, Mary drew a deep breath and fell into a troubled sleep. It was nearly morning.

Chapter 22

Another Passover

Years pass quickly when you are getting older, Mary reasoned. It was nearly time for Passover again. She had heard stories of Jesus' work in Judea, not many, and she wasn't sure how much of what she heard was true and how much was overblown. One story came to her that Jesus, only by speaking a word, had made a nobleman's son well in Capernaum.

There was also the troubling rumor that Jesus had spent some time with the Samaritans. *Samaritans are generally despised,* Mary thought. *What will this do for his reputation, respect, and authority? And why is he going to the Samaritans anyway? He is supposed to be king of Israel, not king of the Samaritans! Not only that, but he has been seen speaking to a woman of ill repute who is a Samaritan. And he has gone into the city of Sychar with her. In fact, rumor has it that he has a great following of Samaritans and that they believe that he is indeed the Son of God. But what good does that do, when He is going to be king of Israel?*

Unwanted memories of the Samaritan who had been a Roman soldier, the one who had helped her, filled Mary's mind. Could he be one who believed in her son? He knew the story of Jesus' conception. He seemed to believe before he even knew who Jesus was.

As Mary prepared for the trip to Jerusalem again, these thoughts troubled her. It seemed to her that Jesus simply courted trouble from the religious leaders. She didn't understand it. If he was to be the king in Israel, why didn't he look for approval from these people in positions of power, who had the ability to help his cause so much more?

As she traveled the road between Nazareth and Jerusalem with her sons, she pondered the best way to approach her eldest son. It seemed that he was less approachable, though. No matter what she said, he would smile patronizingly and go ahead with his own plan. She was so afraid that he was laying ground for his own destruction.

Her fears found foundation in the stories that were circulating when she reached Jerusalem. Joseph's cousins with whom she stayed for the Passover could talk of nothing but the miracles Jesus had performed and the Pharisees' and Sadducees' reaction to them. It seemed Jesus had flouted his religious roots so far as to work on the Sabbath and to teach others to do the same. He had gone to the pool of Bethesda, near the sheep market, and on the Sabbath had ordered

Another Passover

a man to pick up his bed and walk.[1] Of course, the miracle was wonderful. The man had been crippled for nearly forty years and he was now well. But Jesus could have done his healing and could have ordered the man to carry his bed on another day. Or the man could simply have left his bed behind and carried it home after the Sabbath hours were over. *No one else would have carried it away on the Sabbath day*, Mary reasoned.

The story was more than rumor. Her host had been in the temple the day the man came into the temple and pointed Jesus out as the one who had healed him. And Jesus said, "Behold, you are made whole. Sin no more, lest a worse thing come unto you."

"The priests are looking for a way to kill Jesus," Nahum told Mary.

"Just because he broke a Sabbath rule?" Mary asked, shocked.

"That," Nahum replied, "and that he is rejecting Joseph as his father."

"What has he said?" Mary interrupted impatiently.

"He claims God is his father and has made himself equal with God."

Oh no! thought Mary, perplexed. Making oneself equal with God in any way was considered blasphemy, and she couldn't believe that Jesus would go so far as to commit it. She feared what might happen to Jesus now. Even she didn't understand exactly what Jesus would have meant by such a statement. She thought that he was going to be taking the steps necessary to become king of Israel, but instead, as Jesus' interactions with the public and the religious leaders went on, she could not see how he was going to turn this around in his favor.

Why? Mary wondered.

Worried as she was, Mary went to the first service of the Passover out of habit. All around her, people spoke of Jesus. Some, having been touched by miracles in their lives, praised him as a great healer. "I'll go anywhere he goes," one woman said to another. "He healed my boy, you know."

"Yes, and my granddaughter was so sick before Jesus came to their house."

But Mary heard the other side too. The troubling stories of blasphemy and the attempts of the rulers to destroy Jesus. Historically, those who claimed such a close relationship with God were stoned. And Jesus didn't just claim a close relationship; he claimed to be equal with God!

A stir in the back of the crowd caught Mary's attention, and word drifted through the women that Jesus was in the outer court. *It isn't enough to court trouble,* Mary thought. *Jesus has to put himself right in the very path of it.*

Mary moved with the crowd, pushing her way toward Jesus, whom she hadn't seen for nearly a year. "The priests have accused him of blasphemy again," someone in the crowd said.

Mary got close enough to hear Jesus' first words.

"The Son can do nothing of himself but what he sees the Father do, for whatsoever he does, these also the Son does likewise. For the Father loves the Son and shows him all things that He

---

1   John 5:1–15

Mary's Story

Himself does, and He will show him greater works than these, so you may marvel. For as the Father raises up the dead and gives life to them, even so the Son will give life to whom he will."[2]

Mary gasped. She admitted she wished Jesus would refrain from saying things that would aggravate the priests to the point of jeopardizing his own influence and safety. She kept anxiously hoping that he would adopt a more tactful approach.

Jesus' next words were even more infuriating to the priests. "The Father judges no man, but has given all judgment to the Son, that all men should honor the Son even as they honor the Father. He who does not honor the Son does not honor the Father who sent him."[3]

Murmurs ran through the crowd. Supporters of Jesus, those whom his miracles had touched, applauded his words, while those who supported the Sanhedrin angrily muttered, "He should be stoned today!"

But Jesus hadn't finished condemning himself in the eyes of the Jewish leaders. "I say to you, he who hears what I say and believes in Him who sent me has everlasting life and shall not come into condemnation, but is passed from death unto life. The hour is coming—and now is—when the dead shall hear the voice of the Son of God, and they who hear shall live. For as the Father has life in Himself, so hath He given to the Son to have life in himself and has given me the authority to execute judgment also, because I am the Son of man."[4]

The mutterings of the crowd grew darker and louder. "Don't be surprised," Jesus continued. "The hour is coming when all who are in their graves shall hear my voice and shall come forth; they who have done good, to the resurrection of life, and they who have done evil to the resurrection of damnation. I myself can do nothing. As I hear, I judge. And my judgment is just because I seek not my own will but the will of the Father, who has sent me."[5]

The crowd was silent. *Are they shocked at the boldness of Jesus' words?* Mary wondered and trembled.

"If I bear witness of myself, my witness isn't true," Jesus continued. "There is another who bore witness of me, and I know that the witness that he said of me is true." Jesus looked pointedly at the priests standing near. "You sent spies to John, and he bore witness to the truth. But I don't need testimony from man. I say these things so that you might be saved. John was a burning and a shining light. But I have a greater witness than that of John. The works that the Father has given me to finish, the same works that I do, bear witness of me, that the Father has sent me."[6]

Jesus paused, scanning the faces of the people in the crowd. Mary was aware of the moment when Jesus spotted her in the crowd. "The Father Himself, who has sent me, has borne witness of me." His eyes burned into Mary's very soul. But at his next words, his eyes seemed to burn

---

2 See John 5:19
3 See John 5:23
4 See John 5:24–27
5 See John 5:28, 29
6 See John 5:30–45

Another Passover

into those of a priest standing nearby. "You have neither understood His voice at any time nor seen His shape."

Mary recalled vividly the voice of God at the riverbank when John had baptized Jesus, "This is my beloved Son." She had seen the dove descend on Jesus' head and then remembered the priest's words. "You're hallucinating," he had jeered at those around him. "Thunder and lightning, and you think you hear the voice of God."

Jesus' next words seemed to burn themselves into Mary's own heart. "You do not have the Word of God abiding in you, for whom He has sent, you believe not. Search the Scriptures, for in them you think you have eternal life, but they are what testifies of me."

Sadness filled Jesus' voice as he continued speaking. "You will not come to me so that you might have life." He paused as if in introspection, and the crowd moved restlessly.

Jesus' voice took on new strength as he continued speaking. "I receive not honor from men. But I know you, that you do not have the love of God in you. I have come in my Father's name and you do not receive me. If another shall come in his own name, him you will receive. How can you, who seek honor of one another and do not seek the honor that comes from God only, believe?

"Do not think that I will accuse you to the Father? There is another who accuses you—Moses. You trust him, but had you believed Moses, you would have believed me, for he wrote of me. If you do not believe Moses' writings," Jesus voice sounded defeated, "how shall you believe my words?"

The rest of Passover passed in a haze for Mary. Even the remarks the people she stayed with made about Jesus passed over her head. Jesus came to see her, but she couldn't respond to him the way she should. Every waking minute, and sometimes in her dreams, Jesus' words burned into her soul. "Search the Scriptures. Had you believed Moses, you would believe me, for he wrote of me." Mary determined to get out the old scrolls when she got home and re-study the prophecies about Jesus.

Chapter 23

The Nazareth "Reception"

Mary was surprised when it was time to leave that Jesus and his disciples planned to travel with her. "I am returning to Galilee," he told her. "My work in Judea is finished. I have been rejected by the rulers of the people, and more and more, people want to be near me for what I do, not for who I am." Mary could relate to that, and she was thankful that Jesus was coming home. In fact, it raised her spirit so well that the journey back to Nazareth was very pleasant indeed.

The following Sabbath Jesus attended his hometown synagogue with his mother. The priest, new since Jesus had been there last, had heard of Jesus' reputation as a teacher and asked him, as a visitor, to read the Scripture for the day. He handed Jesus the scroll of Isaiah and indicated which text he wanted him to read. Jesus read flawlessly in the original language, and the interpreter repeated it in Aramaic.

"The Spirit of the Lord is upon me, because he hath anointed me to preach the gospel to the poor; he has sent me to heal the brokenhearted, to preach deliverance to the captives, and recovering of sight to the blind, to set at liberty them that are bruised, to preach the acceptable year of our Lord."[1]

Quietly Jesus went back to his seat beside his brothers. All eyes in the synagogue were on him. Mary felt a quiet pride in the son she had raised with the help of Joseph and God. And then Jesus opened his mouth.

"This day is this scripture fulfilled," he said.

People stirred restlessly. "Isn't this Joseph's son?" a woman near Mary questioned her neighbor. "I didn't think carpenters were so well-educated." Mary smiled mistily at Jesus.

Again he spoke. "You will surely say to me this proverb, 'Physician, heal thyself.' You've no doubt heard what I have done in Capernaum, and you want me to do the same thing here."

Nods and murmurs greeted his statement.

"But let me tell you a truth. No prophet is accepted in his own country. There were many widows in Israel in the days of Elijah when the heavens were shut up three years and six months, when great famine spread throughout all the land, but Elijah was sent to none of them. Instead he was sent to Sarepta, to Sidon, to a woman who was a widow. And there were many lepers in

---

1   Luke 4:18, 19, cf. Isa. 61:1, 2.

The Nazareth "Reception"

Israel during the time of Elisha, the prophet, and none of them was cleansed, except Naaman, the Syrian."

At his words the pleased nods turned to mounting anger. Mary's heart plummeted. *Oh, God, why does he do this?* she prayed. *Can't you stop him from courting trouble? Why will he constantly flout convention? Why will he constantly try to make people angry and stir them up? If he is going to stir them, why not incite them against the Romans? Oh, God, do something about him. He talks to You all the time. Can't You help him do better?*

But God didn't do anything.

"Take him to the hill," a man shouted.

The congregation rose in unison. Some of the men grabbed Jesus by his robe and thrust him through the door of the synagogue into the street. As he rose to his feet, more men fell on him. They hustled him out of town and up to the bluff overlooking the Valley of Rocks. Shouting all the way, the men dragged Jesus, who seemed not to resist, while the women urged them on. Mary followed helplessly, while Jesus' brothers tried ineffectually to stop the riot.

Tears ran down Mary's face, and she watched the people around her picking up stones. Jesus would be killed after all! After all they had done to protect him as a baby, he would die as she should have died when she first realized she had him in her womb—stoned at the base of the cliff. *Why wasn't Joseph still here? The angel always talked to Joseph about Jesus' safety. The angels never warn me. Nor do they warn Jesus, evidently. Why wouldn't the angels warn me? Why does Jesus try to make people angry at him?* She covered her face with her hands, weeping. Jude ran up and wrapped his arm around her.

"It's all right, Mother," he said.

"What do you mean it's all right? They are going to throw your brother from the cliff and stone him, and you say it's all right?"

"No, they're not! Look!" Mary peered at the crowd through her tears. People milled around looking confused, especially the men who only moments before had Jesus in their hands.

"What happened?" Mary felt as confused as the men looked.

"Jesus just disappeared," Jude said excitedly. "They had him to the edge of the cliff, and he just disappeared."

Mary clutched Jude's arm. "They threw him over!" she exclaimed, fear overtaking her entire being. She thought her heart would break. She began to run toward the cliff, but Jude grabbed her and pulled her back, laughing.

"No, Mother. They didn't throw him over. Jesus just disappeared!"

"Let me go!" she ordered. Gathering her skirts in one hand, she ran toward the cliff. No one stopped her. They all seemed a bit dazed. She ran to the edge and peered over, expecting to see the broken body of her firstborn son among the rocks, but there was nothing there. She turned around and looked at the people, then through the thinning crowd toward where Jude stood, still

Mary's Story

calm and composed.

Then it hit her. Jesus had got away. Somehow he had thwarted the plans of the people he had so angered, and he was safe, even now. Relief flooded through her. But if he was safe, where was he? She ran back to where Jude stood. Grabbing his arm, she panted, "Where did he go?"

"I don't know," Jude admitted, letting out a chuckle. "But did you see the priests' faces?"

Mary looked about at the dazed crowd. The priests seemed especially surprised at the loss of their quarry. "But where did he go?" she repeated.

"Maybe he's back home," Jude suggested. Without another word, Mary grabbed her skirts again and ran toward her house. Gasping for air as she neared the workshop, she stopped and grasped the corner for support, catching her breath. Then she saw him.

"Why do you do it?" she asked desperately.

Jesus smiled. "You still don't understand, do you, Mother. I must be about my Father's business." He kissed her forehead gently. "I'm leaving. I will see you later."

"But where are you going?"

"Capernaum, first," he replied, "then to the other cities of Galilee, wherever I may teach in a synagogue. I must be about my Father's business."

Mary grabbed him in a fierce embrace, this son whom she didn't really understand, then let him go. "Shalom," she said. "God go with you."

Jesus gave her an enigmatic smile. "You still don't understand, Mother." He turned and walked away, while she remained where she was and watched. At the end of the street he turned and waved. He was gone again.

As before, stories of Jesus filtered back to Nazareth. Mary was astonished when she heard how a demoniac in one of the synagogues accosted Jesus, and she wondered anew when she learned he had cast out the demons and made the man totally whole and well again.[2] She heard how Peter's mother-in-law was ill and had been made well by Jesus' touch and words; how that same evening hundreds of people had come to Peter's house and Jesus had made them well.[3] She heard how he healed a leper and how a paralyzed man had been lowered through a roof to be healed by Jesus.[4]

She also heard how Jesus baited the Pharisees at every turn, how he antagonized those in power everywhere he went. When he healed the paralytic, it was said he didn't do it as before. Since there were priests present, he deliberately said, "Your sins are forgiven; go and sin no more." Then he had asked the priests whether it was easier to forgive sins or heal someone. "So you may know I have the power to forgive sins," he said as he turned to the crippled man and told him, "I say to you, rise, take up your bed, and walk."

It seemed he went out of his way to confront the religious leaders, such as, for instance,

---

2   See Mark 1:21–28; Luke 4:31–37
3   See Luke 4:38–41
4   See Mark 1:40–45

The Nazareth "Reception"

when he led his disciples through a grain field on the Sabbath, threshing the grain in their hands and eating it for a meal.[5]

And then he called a publican to be one of his special followers, his group of hand-picked men.[6] Mary had a difficult time making sense of it all and often felt sick in her stomach. She couldn't stop worrying about what all this commotion and controversy would come to. She couldn't imagine how it could all possibly settle down enough for Jesus to be successful in his mission. *Doesn't he see? Doesn't he know*, mused Mary, *that kind of person will do nothing to help his real cause? Has he forgotten the reason he was born? Doesn't he know he is to be the king of Israel? Does he think I raised him to be a king only to stand by and watch him walk away from it and throw away the opportunities? He had better think again!*

Then came the other stories, about the centurion's servant who was healed by a word,[7] the two men who were blind and received sight, and another man filled with demons[8] and also blind who was completely healed. Then came the story of the widow whose only son had died. Some rumors said Jesus had stopped the funeral procession; others said he had showed up right after the boy died. Whatever the circumstances, they all agreed that Jesus had indeed resurrected the boy.[9] Jude had brought that particular story home with a wistful afterthought. "Why couldn't he raise father to life?"

Joses and Simon scoffed at the idea, but a germ of hope grew in Mary's heart. Why not? She sat silently for a moment, twisting the edge of her head covering between her fingers and thumb.

At last she said, quietly, "We are going to see him."

"Who? Jesus?" Joses asked.

"Yes, Jesus," Simon answered in disgust. "Who do you think we have been talking about?"

"Do you know where he is now?" Joses asked. Mary shook her head.

"One of you will have to find out where he is and where he will be going next," Mary said, "so that we may catch up to him." She looked at each of her sons. "Which of you wishes to do it?"

"I'll go," Jude answered.

Jude spent the rest of the day questioning travelers who entered Nazareth. Some of them had seen Jesus, but it had been so long before, that the information was useless now. Others had never seen him at all. At last, one man came into Nazareth from Nain. Jude asked his question. "Have you seen Jesus?"

"The rabbi?" the man answered. "Only two days ago. There's a large crowd following him now. Did you know Chuza's wife is following him and supporting him with her money?"

"Chuza's wife?" Jude could hardly credit it.

---

5   See Mark 2:23–28
6   See Mark 2:13–14
7   See Luke 7:1–10
8   See Matt. 8:28–33
9   See Luke 7:11–17

Mary's Story

"Yes, man. You know who Chuza is—Herod's chief steward. Next to Herod, he must be the richest man in the nation. His wife, Joanna, is supporting Jesus. Of course, there are other women following him, too. There's Mary, the Magdalene, who had seven devils cast out of her, they say, and Susanna, and there are a lot more I can't name. Then there are those twelve men from up around the Sea of Galilee, who are his special disciples. Those few seem to have the best access to him. If you want his ear, you are more likely to get it if you come in contact with one of those people."

"But where did you see him?"

"In Nain, of course. He's been there for a few days, but I heard rumors that he was going to come this direction. He is supposed to visit Exaloth next, and I expect him to go there tomorrow at the latest."

"Thank you," Jude breathed. He hurried home to give his mother the news. Jesus would be less than five miles away on the morrow. It would be easy to see him.

Chapter 24

Panthera[1]

Early the next morning, Mary and her sons began the short journey to see Jesus. Hope filled Mary's heart. *If he had resurrected the widow's son, surely he would resurrect his own father,* Mary thought.

She still wasn't sure that the story was true. But her hope buoyed her spirits. When they reached town, it was obvious something important was happening. As they neared the center of town, they began to hear Jesus' name spoken more and more. The crowd grew thicker as they traveled. At last they could go no further.

Joses tried to make room for them. "Let us pass," he ordered. "We are the brothers of the rabbi, and this is his mother." It worked for a short time. But then the crowd thickened to the point that they could not get any closer.

"We have to see him," Mary exclaimed. "If he knew we were here, he would be sure we got to see him. He wouldn't turn away his own mother and brothers." A woman standing nearby heard Mary's words. She signaled to one of the men closest to Jesus who whispered in Jesus' ear.

"Who is my mother, and who are my brothers?" Jesus asked the crowd. He waved his hand toward the motley group around him, those disciples he had chosen from the fishing fleets, the dirty peasants he had picked up in his travels, the women (including a prostitute, Mary had heard, and the wife of Herod's steward, Chuza, among others). "These are my mother and brothers," he announced. His words crushed Mary's heart. She nearly turned away, but then Jesus spoke again, looking directly into her eyes. "My mother and my brethren are those who hear the word of God and do it," he said.

Mary felt somewhat ill at Jesus' statement. *When have I not obeyed God? When I knew I was carrying him? When I couldn't help but be critical of his choice of company and friends?* Mary's heart ached because to her, Jesus was still her son and one she loved with all her heart. She thought about her and Joseph's cooperation with God to bring Jesus into the world, her close involvement with Jesus' every breath and move; her heart could not help but feel heavy when Jesus, fully occupied with his divine mission she had a difficult time grasping, seemed so detached now. She

---
1 With the exception of Panthera's role in the story, the events and Jesus' sayings in this chapter are based on Luke 8.

couldn't help but feel abandoned. But she ruminated on Jesus' words, took them to heart, and searched her own soul to make sure her heart was right with God, that she, too, was still hearing God's word and doing it.

In the midst of Mary's thoughts, Jesus returned to his narrative. "No man, upon lighting a candle, covers or puts it under a bed but sets it on a candlestick so that those who enter in may see the light. For nothing is secret that shall not be made manifest and neither is anything hidden that shall not be known and come to light." He turned to look at his mother and brothers as he spoke the last words of his sermon. "Take care, therefore, how you hear, for to the one who has, more will be given, and those who do not have will lose even that which they think they have."

Jesus moved away from his family, and the crowd closed in around him. Tears filled Mary's eyes. *What does he mean? Has he rejected us? How could he choose a prostitute and a bunch of fishermen over his own mother and brothers? What kind of hold do these people have on my precious Jesus? And why, oh why, doesn't he make friends with those in high places who can help him fulfill the promise God made so long ago? He is the Messiah, meant to be the king of Israel, and he is going about it all wrong!*

"Mary," a man's voice interrupted her thoughts. She turned. He stood behind her, dressed in some of the finest garments she had seen. His hair was beginning to silver, and his smile was open and friendly. His face looked familiar, but Mary couldn't think of a name.

"Don't you remember me?" There was something about that voice, but she couldn't place it.

Slowly Mary shook her head, blinking the tears from her eyes. The boys were looking on in bewilderment. They had come to ask Jesus to raise their father to life, and here was this strange man and Jesus had totally rejected his family.

The man smiled. She remembered the smile but couldn't remember where she had seen it. "Thank you," the man said.

She frowned. Was everyone talking in riddles today? "What do you mean?"

"For giving Jesus to the world."

"He won't have anything to do with his own mother and brothers," is all Mary could say with bitterness as she wondered for a moment who this somewhat familiar person was.

The man shook his head. "Did you forget that story you told me?" he continued. "What did the angel tell you about the baby you carried?"

Mary took another long look at the man. "Panthera?" she gasped. He smiled. "But—"

"I gave up soldiering. Forty years in the saddle in all kinds of weather for Herod was enough." He sobered. "Do you remember what the angel told you?"

"Of course I remember what the angel told me!" said Mary. Mary felt cross, and her words came out that way. And yet Mary couldn't understand what Panthera was driving at.

"Tell me the story again."

Mary gave him a withering look. She looked at her sons for support, but they were looking at Panthera, interested, wondering. "Joses," Mary spoke sharply. She would have him take her away right now. He looked at her.

"Tell us, Mother. You used to tell us when Jesus was home and growing up, but you haven't told the story for a long time. I wonder if Jude even remembers it, and I know James hasn't heard it."

Mary thought back. She had stopped telling the story after Jesus had been left in the temple. She and Joseph had both thought after that incident that it might be better if Jesus didn't have quite as much of a reminder of his mission. Perhaps, in not telling it, they had lost sight of why Jesus was here. Maybe that's why Jesus, too, seemed to have lost sight of the mission his life was meant to have. Remorse filled her. *How can we have been so blind?*

"Tell us the story, Mother," Jude added his pleas to his brother's.

So she told the story again. "I was praying one day," she began, "when the angel came. It has been the dream of every woman since Eve to be the mother of the Messiah. And when the angel came, he told me I had found favor with God. He told me I would have a baby boy and that I should name him Jesus. He said he would be great and be called the Son of the Highest, and that he would be given the throne of David. The angel said Jesus would reign over the house of Jacob forever, and there will be no end to his kingdom." She paused, remembering. "When the angel appeared to your father," she said slowly, "he said again that we should name the baby Jesus, for he would save his people from their sins."

She shot a questioning look at Panthera, and he nodded. "At the river, Mary, when Jesus was baptized," he prodded, "do you remember what happened there?"

"You were there?" Mary questioned.

Panthera nodded again.

Mary drew a long, steadying breath. "After Jesus was baptized, there was a voice from heaven and a dove that lit on his head."

"And the voice said …" Panthera prompted.

"This is my beloved son—"

"God's son, Mary," Panthera sounded very serious. "Jesus isn't your son, like these young men here. You were only given Jesus for a little while. He is really God's son. "And you must believe that to have life eternal. That is why he is here, Mary."

"I know he is God's son." Irritation made Mary's words sharper than she intended. "But the angel said he will be king of Israel, that he will inherit the throne of David, that his kingdom will last forever. But the angel didn't say anything about eternal life." Mary shook her head. "You must be mistaken, Panthera."

Panthera reached out and took Mary's hand. Strange that she remembered how his hand felt, Mary thought. If he had done nothing but take her hand, she would have known it was him. "Think about it, Mary," he said gently. "It was nice to see you again."

Mary's Story

He started to walk away. But suddenly Mary remembered. "Panthera," Mary called to him. He turned back. "You know that in the temple," Mary began, feeling embarrassed, but he needed to know. "In the temple Jesus is listed as your son."

Panthera looked stunned. "How … ?"

Bitterly Mary explained. "The priest from Nazareth saw us together. He was the one who circumcised Jesus. He refused to put him down as Joseph's son. He wrote your name in the record and listed Jesus as an illegitimate child." She drew a deep, shuddering breath. "Jesus has had to live with that all his life," she said. "Stay away from him. Don't make it harder for him. He will be king one day."

"Oh, Mary," said Panthera compassionately. "You still don't understand. Think. Really think about the angel's message. You will call his name Jesus, for he will save his people—and he is saving all people, Mary, not just Jews—from their sins."

Panthera raised his hand as he had so many years before. "Good-bye, Mary."

Chapter 25

A Head on a Silver Platter

The next Sabbath Mary was surprised to see Jesus in the synagogue again. He spent most of the day teaching, not stopping with just reading a text and expounding on it. His ability to quote and interpret the Scriptures for the people astounded most of them. As Mary drew near, she was surprised again at the comments.

"Isn't this Mary's son?" some asked. "I thought he was a carpenter. How did he become a rabbi? Isn't this Mary's son?"

"Yes," another replied. "And he has all those brothers; they're all carpenters. You know them, Simon, Joses, Jude, James."

"Yes and his sisters; they live right here in Nazareth. What makes him think he knows so much?"

Mary edged around the room, listening to the comments but remembering, as well, Panthera's words. "He is the son of God, Mary. He isn't your son. He isn't your son. He isn't your son…" The words rang like a litany in her ears.

Late in the afternoon, Jesus announced he would heal those who believed. Mary thought nothing could surprise her anymore, but when Cleophas and Mary went up to Jesus, and with a few words he straightened Cleophas' broken legs and healed Mary of the infirmity she had carried for over thirty years, Mary didn't know what to think. She hadn't said anything to Cleophas and Mary about Jesus and God since the summer Jesus turned twelve, since the time they had lost track of him in the temple. *Have I really lost sight of Jesus' mission? Have I been proud to be the mother of the Messiah and not really listened to what Jesus said about himself?* she wondered.

She shook her head. *No, I don't think so. Panthera's understanding might be different, but the angel said to me that Jesus would inherit the throne of David, after all.*

Jesus healed a few others who came to him, but not many came, and at last he walked over to where Mary stood watching. "Hello, Mother," he said. A smile wreathed Mary's face. He hadn't rejected her. He was still her son.

"Hello, son," she replied.

"I bring you some bad news," Jesus said sadly. "Maybe you need to sit down." He looked so serious that Mary felt a sudden chill.

Mary's Story

Carefully she sat on the bench he indicated, one he had made himself for the synagogue while he was still at home. "What is it?"

"John," he said.

Mary clutched his arm. "What has happened to John?"

"Herod has put him in jail for condemning his lifestyle. You know Herod took Herodias from his brother, Phillip, and married her himself."

"But that is wrong. Herod should know that is a sin."

"Herod does know," Jesus replied. "That's why he hasn't done anything worse to John. He knows John is a holy man, and he has changed his life in many ways after listening to John.

"But Herodias hates John, and she hates his condemnation of what she and Herod have done. She will find a way to kill him."

"Oh, surely not, Jesus," Mary gripped Jesus' forearm. "Even she wouldn't go so far as to kill a prophet of God."

"She will," Jesus replied. He patted his mother's hand were it lay on his arm. "I'm sorry to have to tell you about it, Mother, but I knew you hadn't heard." He glanced around the room. "I must go again. I have done as much as I can here," he said with a somewhat grim smile. "A prophet is without honor in his own country, and among his own kin, and in his own house." He gave her a searching look, and Mary lowered her eyes.

Maybe as a prophet, Jesus should be more honored, Mary thought, *but after all, I have cared for him as a child. I knew him better and more intimately than any other person on earth. And I do honor him as a prophet and a rabbi and a king. The people who live here in this town have never really accepted Jesus as anyone special. They have never accepted the idea that Jesus is the Messiah.* Until today, she had believed that Cleophas and Mary would never accept Jesus as anything more than her son. She had always been thankful that they had finally included him in the family.

Jesus gave Mary's hand a slight squeeze. "I must go," he repeated. She knew better by now than to reprove him for traveling on the Sabbath. She had heard that one time he said, "The Sabbath was made for man, not man for the Sabbath. Therefore the Son of man is Lord also of the Sabbath."[1] He was baiting the Pharisees.

Mary kept her eyes to the floor, but heard the comments and good-byes of those around her until he was gone.

Simon brought her the rest of the news about John. Herodias had gotten her way, after all. The palace had thrown a great feast for Herod's birthday. All the nobles of his kingdom gathered for days of feasting and celebration. One evening, Simon told her, Herod had asked his niece, and step-daughter, the sensuous, beautiful Salome, to dance for the men. She had done it, and done it so well that Herod offered her whatever she wanted.

"Her mother coached her," Simon told Mary. "That woman is so evil."

---
1   Mark 2:27

A Head on a Silver Platter

"What did she ask for?"

"The head of John on a silver platter." Simon's words fell into a black pit of silence. He glanced at his brothers, who had come in to hear his news. Mary felt as though the world had dropped out from under her. John was as dear to her as her own boys. She wrapped her arms around her body as if to ward off the chill that came from deep inside her somewhere. Soundlessly, she rocked to and fro.

Only when Joses wrapped his arms around her own, rocking with her grief, did she cry the deep wail of one truly bereft, far from the false wail of hired mourners. "He's too young," she said. Then, "Herod could have hurt me no more if he had really managed to kill Jesus. I'm so glad his parents aren't alive to see this day."[2]

For several days Mary went in a fog. The rest of the family kept up on what news they heard about Jesus. When Jesus heard about John's death, he went to his sanctuary, the wilderness. But even there, the crowds of people followed him. Five thousand men were counted. The women and children, who had not been counted, came to him, and he healed their sick, and in the evening, when the disciples would have sent them away to find food, Jesus fed them by a miracle of producing enough food for all of them from five loaves of barley bread and two small fishes.[3]

The story came that the disciples had taken a boat out on the Sea of Galilee and that a storm had come up. James came home with the story that Jesus had stilled the storm. James had been in another boat that had almost been swamped, and Jesus had stood up and said, "Peace, be still."[4]

"We were in the middle of the lake when that happened," James said. "And we were at the other side when he finished talking. It was strange."

He said he had seen Jesus walk on the water of the lake out to a fishing boat. And even Peter walked on the water a little bit. It didn't last; something changed, so he almost drowned, but Jesus rescued him, and they went back to the boat. Mary wondered why James or Jude couldn't walk on the water. Why didn't he show the same favors to his brothers that he did to that rough fisherman? But she had learned not to say so. James and Jude were so besotted with Jesus and his lifestyle that they defended him and his actions with undying fervor. They told her more than once that she didn't understand what Jesus was doing.

They are right there, Mary thought. *Jesus is supposed to become king, and I certainly don't understand how his lifestyle will accomplish that purpose.*

And she heard the story of the pigs. Even Mary had to admit that was oddly funny and disturbing at the same time. It was right after the storm. James told her that it happened in the country of the Gergesenes. Two men were possessed with demons. They were so fierce that no

---

2   The story about the death of John the Baptist can be found Matt. 14, Mark 6, and Luke 3.
3   See Matt. 14
4   See Mark 6:45–52

Mary's Story

one could even go past the tombs without being run off. In fact, someone had tried to chain them up, but they broke the chains and went into the wilderness. Now they lived in the tombs.

So they came out and said, "What have we to do with you, Jesus, you Son of God? Have you come to torment us before the time?" Jesus asked their name, and they said, "We are Legion."

"I guess there was a legion of devils in the two men," James said. "And then they asked if, since there were so many of them, they might go into the herd of swine that were feeding over there, instead of into the sea. Jesus said, 'Yes,' and as soon as they heard it they went into the swine. Well, the pigs went into the sea and drowned in the water. And the men immediately returned to their right senses."[5]

"I hope they put clothes on," Mary said, thinking of the pigs all drowning in the sea.

"Oh, yes," James answered. "But we couldn't stay. The people in that place were so sorry to see him, they asked Jesus to leave."

When word came that Jesus had had another confrontation with the Pharisees, Mary shook her head. Again he had flouted convention, by not washing his hands the way the law required before eating food. Jude told her that one. "He says it isn't what goes into a man that defiles him," Jude reported gleefully, "but what comes *out* of him."[6]

"Don't be vulgar," Mary admonished her son.

"I'm not," Jude defended himself. "Jesus explained it to us. He said what you eat goes though the body and is cast *out* by your digestive system, but those things which come *out* of the mouth came from the heart, and they defile a person. He said that *out* of the heart come evil thoughts, murders, adulteries, fornications, thefts, false witness, and blasphemies, and these are the things that defile a person, not eating with unwashed hands."[7]

The next time Mary heard of Jesus, the story reached her that he had been on the coasts of Tyre and Sidon and healed the daughter of a Canaanite woman.[8] People were saying he had made a feast for another 4,000 people who came to him for healing there.[9] Mary thought that being able to feed his people with few resources would be a definite advantage for a king.

Next she heard he was in Magdala, where he had a confrontation with the Sadducees, then in Caesarea Philippi. Word came that he had been in Galilee, and Mary couldn't understand why Jesus had not stopped at home. He had always come to see her when he was in Galilee before. But she understood that Jesus was moving fast from place to place. From Galilee he had gone again to Capernaum, where the tax collectors accosted the disciples for tribute money. Word was that Jesus had sent his disciple Peter fishing for the required coin—literally. Peter found the

---

5   See Matt. 8:27–29
6   See Matt. 15:11
7   See Matt. 15:11–20
8   See Mark 7:25–30
9   See Mark 8:1–10

A Head on a Silver Platter

money in the mouth of the first fish he caught.[10]

From there Jesus traveled to the border of Judea beyond the Jordan River, where he was followed by great multitudes of people, and the Pharisees again baited him, trying to get him to make a false step so they could accuse him of something, James said when he came home for a visit. Mary reflected that Jesus had asked for that treatment from them. She wondered when he would stop the game of baiting the Jewish leaders.

James also brought the report that Mrs. Zebedee had asked Jesus to let her two sons, James and John, sit beside him on his throne.[11] Mary was aghast. If anyone should sit with Jesus on his throne, it should be his own brothers! But James said Jesus had turned down anyone who might even think of the position again. "He told Mrs. Zebedee that it wasn't his choice who would sit on his right hand or on his left," James said. "He said his Father would make the choice."

"Then he said something very strange, Mother," James continued. "He said that whoever wanted to be great should be a minister and whoever wanted to be chief among his disciples should be a servant. He said he was going to give his life a ransom for many."[12]

Mary frowned. *What could Jesus mean by that remark?*

"Oh, by the way, Mother," James concluded. "Jesus was in Jericho when that happened, but he left there to go to Jerusalem. I understand he is going from Jerusalem to Bethany, to Mary Magdalene's house. I understand there's going to be a reformed prostitute there, too.'

"There's no such thing as a reformed prostitute," Mary said, "I have never met one or heard of one, at least. Can't Jesus see how people use him? Why does he insist on surrounding himself with such common, coarse, vulgar people? You just be careful, James. Ah, well, if he is going to Bethany, he is going early to Passover."

"I'd like to go in the morning and join him," said James, ignoring his mother's warning. "Would you object to an early trip to Jerusalem?"

"No," Mary replied pensively. "I'll have more time to visit. I never have enough time to visit during Passover."

---

10 See Matt. 17:24–27
11 See Matt. 20:20–24
12 See Matt. 20:25–28

VIII

A Week of Ups and Downs

Chapter 26

The Parade

The early trip to Jerusalem for the Passover proved more interesting than Mary ever dreamed it would be. They took the road south along the Jordan River, as usual, passing through Jericho on the way.

Mary always felt nervous on the road that connected Jericho and Jerusalem. The Zealots had become more bold of late and focused their efforts and activities on the stretch between Jerusalem and Jericho. Since more people traveled that road with money bags, the pickings for their cause were much greater. Merchants and businessmen were never safe there.

They had been on the road for five days when they stopped for the night in Jericho. Early the next morning, they started out again. James wanted to see his mother safely settled with their relatives before returning to Bethany to join Jesus. Only a few miles into the journey, they were met by soldiers beating a newly imprisoned group of zealots into submission.

"What is your name?" the centurion asked persistently as they beat one man, obviously the leader. At first he refused to answer, and Mary cringed for him each time the whip descended to his shoulders. Finally, the man answered. "Bar Abbas."

Mary looked at James. The shock on his face was plain. "Son of Papa?" she whispered.

"I am the Messiah," Bar Abbas shouted. "You can't do this to the Messiah," but the soldiers laughed and did it. Tying Bar Abbas' hands and feet, they threw him over the back of a horse like a sack of meal.

The centurion glanced at the travelers. *Nobody special,* he decided. *No one I should apologize to for the hold-up. They should be thankful I got this brigand out of the way.* The soldiers cantered off with their prisoners, and Mary and James continued their journey, turning away from the river as they went toward Jerusalem.

Just before Jerusalem lay Bethany, and James took time to go to the house of the Magdalenes. Mary, mother of Jesus, was a little surprised that he knew where the house was, but she reflected that James had to have visited this woman with Jesus several times. She still couldn't help but dislike Jesus' association with Mary Magdalene. *What possible good can she be to Jesus as he ascends to the throne of David?*

They approached the house. But there was no one there. The house was empty. And what

Mary's Story

seemed even stranger, few people roamed the streets. "There must be something happening in Jerusalem," James surmised.

As Mary and James neared the city, they heard a mob shouting. In some alarm Mary drew nearer to James. *We shouldn't have come,* she thought. She had seen enough people killed in riots in Jerusalem that were quashed by Herod's men. Another riot would not change anything or be dealt with differently. It would only create one more bad memory for her, but as they drew nearer, she realized that she was hearing singing. There in front of her, she saw the crowd. People laying palm branches on the road, as well as their coats for a donkey to walk on. Not just any donkey—a white donkey, royalty's steed. A king was making his declaration.

Her heart nearly stopped. All the years she and Joseph had worked with Jesus grooming him for just this, and now someone else— She remembered the young man the soldiers had been beating, Bar Abbas, Son of Papa, who thought he was the Messiah. Who was this person?

"It's Jesus," James breathed beside her.

Mary looked carefully. It was Jesus! Triumph replaced fear. At last he was doing the thing he had been born to do. In the time-honored tradition of Jewish kings, Jesus was entering the capital city of the kingdom. He was declaring his kingship.[1] *So this is where the whole town of Bethany is,* Mary thought. They had picked up people all along the way, from the looks of it. Crowds of men, women and children lay their clothes or palm branches on the road in front of the donkey while singing and shouting, "Hosanna to the son of David."

While Jesus' progress was hampered by the crowd in front of him, Mary and James had clear access from behind. They hurried to join the other disciples, who crowded around Jesus. Just as they joined the group, Peter shouted, "Blessed be the King that cometh in the name of the Lord; peace in heaven, and glory in the highest."[2] The words of the song, Mary remembered, that the angel had sung.

Pride swelled in Mary's heart as tears of joy spouted from her eyes. *Oh, if only Joseph could see Jesus now. All the years of work, of raising him for this moment. Joseph should be here to share it.*

Some of the Pharisees who were not averse to singing hosannas thought the disciples had gone too far. Stepping up to Jesus, they said, "Master, rebuke thy disciples."

Mary bridled. *Didn't they understand the significance of this parade? Didn't they know that Jesus would free Israel from oppression? Didn't they understand what the disciples were saying?*

Jesus smiled, and pointing to his disciples, said, "I tell you that if these would hold their peace, the stones would immediately cry out."[3]

The procession continued. James joined the other disciples in proclaiming as they went, "Blessed be the King that cometh in the name of the Lord; peace in heaven, and glory in the

---

1 See Matt. 21:1–11; Luke 19:29–44
2 Luke 19:38
3 Luke 19:40

The Parade

highest."

The procession circled the base of the Mount of Olives, coming out on a high point overlooking Jerusalem. There Jesus stopped. The crowd became quiet, waiting for his proclamation of kingship. Those on the fringes who were shouting were shushed by those closer to the king.

Mary thought she would burst with pride. Everything the angels had promised was about to be fulfilled. She would be the mother of the king of Israel whose kingdom would never end. Later Mary would reflect that Jesus never did what she expected him to do. She never ceased to be surprised.

"He's crying," someone said in hushed tones.

In his hour of triumph? Mary looked at James, who shrugged his shoulders.

Then Jesus' words rang out. "Oh, Jerusalem. if you had only known on this day the things that belong to your peace! But now they are hidden from your eyes." Mary could see by the faces of those around her that they were as confused as she was. Jesus continued, "For the days will come upon you when your enemies will cut a trench around you and surround you on every side and shall lay you to the ground, you and your children within you, and they will not leave one stone upon another, because you didn't know the time when I came to visit you."[4]

Mary, holding her breath, waited for more, waited for Jesus to claim kingship, but all she had heard from Jesus was a curse on Jerusalem. *I don't understand it.*

The party was over before it began. Subdued, the people who had been singing and shouting followed Jesus as he wended his way into Jerusalem. He rode directly to the temple, where, as before, he overturned the tables and threw out the money changers, the animals, the caged birds. Jesus scattered money all over the stones as he shouted, "My house is called the house of prayer, but you have made it a den of thieves."[5]

Striding from group to group, Jesus continued to wreak havoc, tipping over tables, scattering money, animals, salesmen.

At each place he shouted the words, "My house is called the house of prayer, but you have made it a den of thieves." He didn't stop until the last money changer, the last salesman, had fled, the last animal and bird was freed, and the last priest prudently stepped out of his way.

During the following week, Jesus took over the temple. Money changers and animal traders stayed away from the temple grounds while he was there. They set up their trade around the edge of the park, grumbling all the while that Jesus had destroyed their business during the busiest week of the year. Just before Passover everyone came to town for sacrifice, most of them from other countries, making their sale of animals a most important adjunct to the holy services. Didn't Jesus know that?

It made it more difficult to inspect the animals the locals brought in too. It was much more

---

4   See Luke 19:41–44
5   See Luke 19:46

Mary's Story

likely that an animal would be sneaked through the gates of the temple that hadn't been inspected and found perfect. Often the locals brought an animal with some tiny flaw, and they had to keep it a while until the sore was healed or the wool was perfect. Didn't the man realize how important their role was?

Yet they dared not exercise their rights in the temple environs. The man was there day and night. The crowds of people who had come for the Passover crowded into the temple courtyard to listen to him preach. Another problem was the loss of the money that Jesus had left scattered all over the courtyard. The poor had picked it up, claiming it as their own, and he had not rebuked them. He knew that thievery was against the Torah, yet he in effect condoned it and had the temerity to call the dealers thieves!

The more money they lost, the more incensed they became. One suggested the priests should confront this man and challenge his authority. After all, there were high priests, rabbis, scribes. The hierarchy of the system had been challenged by a nobody.

The priests agreed. Gathering elders and scribes to go with them, the priests approached Jesus. "Tell us," Ananias the chief priest broke into Jesus' sermon. "By what authority do you do these things? Who is the one who gave you this authority?"

Jesus looked long and hard at Ananias, then let his gaze roam over the other men in the delegation. "I will also ask you one thing; and [you] answer me," he replied. "The baptism of John, was it from heaven, or of men?"[6]

The group shared glances, then moved as one man to discuss their answer. "If we say his authority is from heaven," one man suggested, "he will ask why we don't believe in him." "But if we say his baptism was of men, all the people will stone us, for they are persuaded that John was a prophet," another contended shakily. "We'll tell him we don't know," suggested a third.

And so they told him, "We don't know where John's baptism came from."

And Jesus answered their question. "Then you wouldn't understand." Jesus heaved a deep sigh. "Neither will I tell you by what authority I do these things." He turned his back on them to continue what he was teaching those who came to listen and believe.

Although the priests didn't believe in Jesus' claims that he was equal with God (in fact, they thought them to be blasphemous), they stayed to listen to his next words, anticipating that he would make something of their question. His story to the people was of a man who owned a vineyard. The owner sent three servants to the vineyard, because he had traveled to a far country, to collect the profits from the business. Each servant was beaten and set away with nothing. At last, the owner sent his son, thinking that the husbandmen of the vineyard would respect his son, and give him the moneys due the owner.

But the men reasoned that if they killed the heir, they would have the inheritance, so they did that. James brought the story to his mother, and at the end he said, "Then Jesus said what

---
6 Luke 20:3, 4.

The Parade

he said when he had told people we were not his mother and brothers: 'For to the one who has, more will be given, and those who not have will lose even that which they think they have.'"[7]

"The priests are trying to find a way to turn the people against Jesus," James warned Mary, "and Jesus isn't doing much to curry their favor."

"He never has," she sighed. Fear gripped her chest. "Why won't he co-operate with those in power? Doesn't he see what he is doing to himself?"

"I think he enjoys baiting them," James replied. "Some of them asked him if they should pay taxes to Caesar."[8]

"What did he answer? Is he trying to start a war with the Romans now?"

"He simply asked for a coin. And when he got it, he asked whose picture was on the coin. When they said, 'Caesar's,' he replied, 'Give to Caesar the things that are Caesar's and to God the things that are God's.'"

"Another group tried to trip him up, and he answered them in such a way that they couldn't use his words against him, as well. In fact, he kept it up all afternoon, and just before the end of it, he looked at us and said, "Beware of the scribes, who want to walk in long robes and love to be noticed in the marketplace. They want the highest seats in the synagogue and the chief rooms at feasts, and for a show they make long, loud prayers. But they devour widows' houses, and they shall receive greater damnation."

"Mary sat back with her hand on her throat, her face, white. "When will he learn to keep his mouth shut?" she breathed.

"That's not all," James commented. "A widow came into the temple while he was teaching, and gave him one more chance to taunt the rich men. You know how they make a big show of dropping their offerings in the box so that people will know how much they give."

Mary nodded, feeling faint.

"Well, when the widow came in, she dropped in two mites. Jesus called our attention to her. He said, loud enough for everyone to hear, 'This poor widow has given more than all of them, for all these,' he pointed at the rich men who and just put in their offerings, 'have given of their abundance, but she has put in all that she had. '"[9]

"Is he staying in the temple tonight?" Mary asked, switching the subject, almost unable to handle any more such reports.

James grinned. "No, he's going out to the Mount of Olives at night. People have found out where he sleeps, and before daylight, they gather so that they can see him wake up and hear every word he says."[10]

"Why does he do that?" Mary asked for what seemed like the hundredth time.

---

7   The story of the priests' challenge of Jesus' authority in the temple is found in Luke 20:1–18
8   See Luke 20:22
9   See Luke 20:21–21:4
10   See Luke 21:31, 38

Mary's Story

But there was no answer. Jesus had never done the expedient thing. She had often questioned the rightness of his behavior, but even more so now. *How could he proclaim himself king, as he had by his actions, though not by words, and continue to anger those in the best position to help his goals? What would happen to him because he alienated those he should find favor with?*

Mary didn't have a lot of time to dwell on Jesus' activities, though she found herself thinking of him while she did mundane things like kneading Passover bread, the unleavened cakes Israelites had eaten since Moses had led them from Egypt so many years before. Her cousin Sarah had married Simon, a Jew from Cyrene who had moved back to Jerusalem, and they shared their home with her for the Passover. Simon had two sons, Alexander and Rufus. They welcomed her light hand with the heavy bread. She mixed the special herbs that were to be used to flavor the Passover lamb and helped with the wines that were appropriate for the occasion.

She had hoped that Jesus would spend this Passover with her at her relatives' home, but James brought word that Jesus planned a private Passover feast with his twelve followers. He and Jude would join them in an upper room Jesus hand-picked for the occasion. Mary was left with the satisfaction that her sons were at least following the religious traditions so important to her, even though it was no longer as a family.

She had always loved the traditions of Passover, the songs, readings from Scripture, the rituals involved in slaying and cooking the lamb. Years ago, she knew people still stood for the meal as they had that first night in Egypt, ready to leave at a moment's notice. But time had changed that. There was no reason to plan to leave in a hurry anymore. The meal and all that attended it was relaxed, and, once the formal rituals had been completed, it was time for festivities and family get-togethers.

They had finished the meal and were well into the evening's activities when James, followed by Jude, burst into the room, eyes wild, shouting, "They've taken him! They've taken him away!"

Chapter 27

The Long Night[1]

Later Mary would reflect that she should have been prepared for it, but nothing could have readied her for the news that her precious firstborn son had been arrested by Herod's soldiers. Despair and depression covered her like an ominous dark cloud. She barely heard Simon's questions as he calmed her boys down enough to find out what had happened.

Jesus had taken his disciples to an upper room in Nicodemus' house. There they had eaten the Passover dinner. After the dinner, Jesus had taken them all to the Mount of Olives. He left everyone except Simon Peter, and James and John, the sons of Zebedee. It wasn't unusual for him to take those three with him. Often the others felt he was grooming them for some special place in his kingdom.

James, Jude and the other disciples had been asleep when the soldiers made their way up the path. The noise of their passing had awakened them, and with the others they followed. In the light of the torch they had seen the face of Judas Iscariot leading the soldiers to the place where he knew Jesus would be.

"I didn't think Jesus should trust Judas Iscariot so much," Alexander exclaimed. "Peter mentioned to me once that he thought Judas was stealing from the disciples' money bag."

"Jesus knew he was," James began pacing the room. "The strangest thing about this whole evening was that Jesus told Judas to go and do what he was going to do."

"What?" Rufus exclaimed. "What are you saying?"

"We all knew Jesus tried to incite the Pharisees long ago, but to deliberately send one of his own to betray him doesn't make sense." Simon reasoned, raking his hands through his thinning hair. "Even Jesus wouldn't do that, would he?"

"Evidently he did," James answered, disgusted. "He said during supper that someone would betray him."

Jude spoke up for the first time: "He said it would be the person he gave the sop to."

"John asked him who it would be," James continued. "But we never paid much attention to what Jesus said at that point. He had done so many strange things during the evening. He washed

---

1 With the exception of Panthera's role in the story, the events and Jesus' sayings in this chapter are based on Luke 8.

Mary's Story

our feet like a servant."

"He did what?" Simon said. He had finally become certain, as Mary had, that Jesus was destined to become king of Israel. "What was he trying to prove? No king in his right mind does the work of a servant!"

"I don't know," James replied. "Later he told Judas Iscariot, 'That you do, do quickly.'"

"I thought he was just sending Judas out to buy something for the feast," continued Jude, "or that Judas was going to give an offering from the bag to the poor, as Jesus had often told him to do. Judas went out, and we didn't see him again until we saw him on the path to the garden with the soldiers."

"Judas knew were Jesus would be," Jude said bitterly. "We had often gone there to that place in the garden with Jesus. And there were more than just the soldiers. The priests were with them. Do you remember that old priest from Nazareth?" he said, turning to his mother.

Mary barely nodded, and he continued. "He was there."

"What did Jesus do? Did he run or do a miracle or anything?" Simon could hardly believe Jesus would do nothing to save himself if he were to be the king.

"He asked them whom they were looking for as if he didn't know," James answered, "and when they said, 'Jesus, of Nazareth,' he told them that he was the one, as if they didn't know."

"Then a bright light came, and they fell down like dead men," Jude said.

"Didn't that frighten them? Didn't they know then that they shouldn't bother Jesus?" Simon asked.

"I guess not," James replied. "It happened a second time, and they still didn't seem to notice God was trying to tell them something."

"Ananias was there," Jude said.

"The high priest himself?" Simon could hardly believe it.

"Yes. And you know that servant of his that thinks he's so grand—Malchus?" Jude was warming up to his story. "Peter cut off his ear with his sword," reported Jude with satisfaction in his voice.

"Peter cut off his ear?" asked Simon, eyes wide.

"Yes," James sighed. "And Jesus told him not to fight." James didn't understand his brother's actions at all. "He healed Malchus' ear and told Peter to put his sword away. He said he would fight if his kingdom were of this world but that it was not."

"All those miracles, all the things they have seen him do, but those priests wouldn't accept Jesus as anyone special for any reason at all! Satan has blinded them completely!" James said bitterly. "Jesus asked them then why they had come out at night, like thieves, to take him. He reminded them that he was in the temple every day. They could have taken him in the daylight, and then he said, 'This is your hour, and the power of darkness.'"[2]

---

[2] Luke 22:53

The Long Night

"What happened then?" Simon asked.

"Judas Iscariot kissed Jesus on both cheeks, and Jesus looked at him and asked, 'Why do you betray the Son of man with a kiss?' Then they tied Jesus' hands behind his back like those of a common criminal and led him away," Jude replied.

"Where to?" Simon continued to question.

"I don't know."

"You don't know?"

"We all ran away," James said then hung his head.

But Jude defended their actions: "It would have done no good at all if they had taken all of us," he said.

"I think Peter followed them," James said. "He may come and let us know where they took him."

"We won't wait for Peter," Simon said decisively. "If you young puppies are too frightened to find out where your brother is, I will find out. We must know for your mother's sake, if for no other reason, where he is and what is happening."

For the first time Mary's two sons seemed to notice their mother's white face. They rushed to her side. James put his arms around her and held her close, and Jude ineffectually patted her hands. "Thank you for agreeing to go find Jesus for us," James said to Simon.

With a snort Simon walked away. Those boys had a lot of growing up to do in spite of their ages, he thought.

It didn't take Simon long to locate the group who had taken Jesus. A crowd had gathered around Ananias' house, where a bonfire had been built in the courtyard. In the crowd he saw a white-faced Peter, but with a determined look. He started toward him, when a young girl accosted Peter.

"You were with him; I saw you," she said.

"Lady, I don't know him," Peter replied.

Simon stopped in his tracks. If the big Galilean wasn't recognizing Jesus, there must be something going on.

Avoiding Peter, Simon edged his way through the crowd to where he could see what was happening in Ananias' house. Jesus stood in the center of the large room, a blindfold on his face. The chief priest himself stood in front of Jesus and slapped his face hard. "Prophesy," he mockingly ordered Jesus. "Who struck you?"

Jesus answered nothing.

Some of the others joined in on the fun. Slapping Jesus, they imitated the chief priest; as they continued, some thought up their own remarks. For an hour Simon watched, trying desperately to devise some means to rescue Jesus, but Jesus' followers were so few, and they had run away. Only Simon Peter stood there, and as he thought again to confer with the disciple, he turned just in time to hear another accost him.

"You are one of his disciples," the man said.

Peter swore. "I am not. Do you think I'd be here if I were?"

No help there, Simon was sure. What had happened to the crowds who had followed him for his miracles? Where were those he had fed on nothing? Where were all those he had healed and blessed?

He turned back toward the hall, almost unable to bear the sight yet trying desperately to devise a plan to save Jesus. *Maybe some of the others have returned*, he thought. Turning away from the sickening sight of Jesus being savagely beaten and tormented, Simon sought some of the other disciples. Though he scouted the crowd thoroughly, there was only Peter. The mood was definitely against Jesus.

"About time," one man spoke to his companion as Simon edged by. "Anyone who claims to be the son of God is a lunatic. They should have stopped him long ago, I say. The gullible poor will follow any pervert who comes along. If he does any miracles, it is probably with the power of the devil. He has to be stopped."

Simon reached Peter just in time to see another man approach him. "I'm sure you were with him," the man said. "You are a Galilean."

"You don't know what you're talking about," Peter denied. In the distance a cock crowed. Simon reflected that it was nearly morning. How much of this did they intend to do? How long would they keep beating Jesus? At the sound of the rooster's crow, Peter's head snapped up. Staring above the crowd, he looked intently at Jesus. Ignoring the taunts and slapping hands, Jesus turned his head and stared straight into his disciple's eyes. Peter's face turned red in the firelight. A sick look passed over him. Without another word he turned, buried his face in his hands, and stumbled away into the night.

So much for the tough Galilean, Simon thought. The sun rose slowly while the group in the priest's house continued to abuse Jesus. Simon felt helpless, watching, doing nothing.

Ananias, the priests, the scribes, and the elders finally crowded around Jesus. The abuse stopped, and they led him into the council chambers. Simon crowded in to hear as much as he could.

The question he heard was "Are you the Christ; do you claim to be the Messiah?"

One answer: "If I tell you, you won't believe, and if I ask you questions, you will not answer me. You won't let me go. You will see me later sitting on the right hand of the power of God."

"Are you, then, the son of God?"

"You say that I am."

Ananias looked triumphantly at the others. "Do we need any more witnesses? Everyone here heard him witness against himself with his blasphemy. Let's take him to Pilate."

What is keeping Simon? Mary wondered as she paced back and forth between the door and

The Long Night

the window. There was no thought of sleep that night. Ever since James and Jude had brought the news of Jesus' arrest, she paced. They had encouraged her to sleep, but she had scorned them. *How can they even contemplate sleeping the night away; how can they even think of my sleeping, when I don't know what is happening to my boy?* Mary thought in near disbelief.

Shortly after dawn Simon returned, haggard from his all-night vigil, his steps slow, his grizzled head bowed. Mary ran to meet him, James and Jude not far behind. "Where is Jesus? What have they done to my Jesus?"

Simon wondered how much he should tell her. Her anguish was so great already. She spoke again as if reading his mind. "Not knowing is killing me, Simon. Tell me what you know."

So Simon told her of the long night, the torture, the abuse, the taunts, and of Peter, who had run away with the dawn and the crowing of the cock.

"What are they going to do now?" Jude asked his kinsman.

"They are taking him to Pilate. Someone needs to go and see what is happening," Simon replied.

"I'm going," James said as he ran off.

Simon wrapped his strong arm around Mary's sagging shoulders. "I don't know what is happening," he said to her, "but it's as if Jesus wants it to happen."

"How could anyone want to be abused?" she nearly shouted. "Has he lost his mind? Has he really gone over the edge?"

Chapter 28

Standing in Judgment[1]

James reached Pilate's court in time to hear Pilate say, "I find no fault in this man."

"Why is he in judgment if he has no fault?" James asked a man near him.

"Did you just get here?"

At James' nod, the man replied, "He claims to be king of the Jews and the Son of God. The priests are using the idea of a king of Jews to convince Pilate of sedition. Pilate doesn't care that he claims to be the Son of God."

Because it was Passover, the priests stayed outside the court so they wouldn't be defiled and could still participate in the temple activities of the weekend. Pilate went back into the judgment hall. Knowing he would be ceremonially defiled, James followed. It was more important to him to know what Pilate was going to do to Jesus.

"Are you the king of the Jews?" Pilate asked him.

"Are you asking me yourself or did someone tell you to ask me that?" Jesus questioned in response.

"Your own nation and the priests have sent you to me for judgment. What for? What have you done?"

"My kingdom is not of this world," Jesus replied. "If my kingdom were of this world, then would my servants fight so that I should not be delivered to the Jews." He drew a deep breath as he repeated, "My kingdom is not from here."

"Are you a king, then?" Pilate asked.

"You call me a king," Jesus replied. "I was born for only one reason; I came here only to bear witness to the truth. Everyone who understands truth understands why I am here."

Pilate looked at Jesus' face for a long moment. It seemed obvious to James that the potentate was grappling with Jesus' words. At last, at the end of a long sigh, Pilate muttered, almost to himself, "What is truth?" He turned and went back outside to the priests and the crowd of people who had begun to gather.

"I find no fault at all," he told them.

A voice shouted from the crowd of priests. "He is stirring up all the people. He taught all the

---

[1] The story of the arrest of Jesus and his dialogue with Pilate is found in John 18:28–19:16.

Standing in Judgment

Jews throughout the kingdom, from Galilee to Jerusalem."[2]

"Is he Galilean?" Pilate asked.

"Yes. Jesus of Nazareth," a voice replied.

"Then take him to Herod. He is in his palace here in Jerusalem, and he has jurisdiction over Galilee." Pilate turned and walked away.

James' momentary hope when he heard Pilate say he had found no fault in Jesus was dashed as he heard Pilate order them to take Jesus to Herod. Herod could easily be much harsher. The soldiers pushed Jesus out of the courtroom and into the street and jostled him to Herod's judgment hall; James followed behind. At first Herod seemed put out that they had brought a prisoner so early to his judgment, but when he learned who it was, his attitude changed.

"This is Jesus of Nazareth?" he asked to be sure.

"He is, sir," a priest replied.

"Delighted to meet the fellow," Herod exclaimed. "Jesus of Nazareth, will you do a miracle here? I have heard much of your powers and abilities. You will do a miracle for me. You are able to do so." James thought for sure Jesus would do one small miracle to show Herod his ability and potentially save himself, but Jesus stood there, mute, refusing to do anything.

James couldn't believe that Jesus would do nothing. He started forward as if to remind Jesus that he was signing his death warrant and then remembered that he would find himself destroyed by defending his brother.

Herod began questioning Jesus. Question after question about his work, his supposed sedition, his politics. Jesus answered nothing. The priests made their accusations, dwelling on the fact that Jesus claimed to be king of the Jews. They pointed out that Jesus had no right to claim the title and that he was trying to take away the reigning government. The argument held little interest for Herod. He felt secure in his political position. Without answers, and to mock both Jesus and his accusers, he had his servants bring one of his old robes and placed it over Jesus' shoulders.

"You claim to be king; wear the kingly robes," Herod jeered while his soldiers pointed out that the robe Jesus was wearing was hardly fit for a king, since it was ratty and full of holes. One soldier stuck the point of his sword into a hole in the fabric, cutting it larger. Still, Jesus stood without answer, stoic in his silence.

At last, in disgust at not getting the miracle he sought and not receiving the answers to his many questions, Herod gave up. "Take him back to Pilate and see what He wants to do with him," he said. "I can't find any reason to condemn him."

With a dismissive wave of his hand, Herod disappeared into his private apartments. Deprived of their fun, the soldiers pushed Jesus, who was still wearing the old robe Herod had put on him, out into the crowd.

---

2   See Luke 23:5–7

Mary's Story

The priests surged forward and surrounded Jesus to keep him, James was sure, from escaping. He heard a gasp and turned to see his mother supported by Jesus' disciple John, the son of Zebedee.

Making his way to them, he gave John a hard look, then looked at his mother. "Why are you here? This is no place for you to be." Without waiting for an answer, he turned on John. "Why have you brought my mother here?"

"She insisted on coming," John replied. "Would you have her here with no protection at all? She was coming whether I came with her or not."

James clapped John's shoulder. "You're right. I'm sorry," he replied, then ruefully said, "I know my mother." He took Mary's other arm. "Since you're here, let's see what Pilate decides *this* time."

"What has happened? Why is he here?" Mary questioned.

James told her about Pilate's first court. "They have found no reason to condemn him," he said, "but the priests are determined to have him killed, and from the sound of the crowd, they have most of the people here on their side."

"Have the people forgotten so soon how Jesus preached and healed?" Mary asked.

"Perhaps these are the ones who don't care," John replied. "Maybe they just want to be on the winning side."

By then they had reached Pilate's court again. At the demand of the priests, the soldiers again took Jesus inside. "Stay here," James ordered. "I am already ceremonially defiled. I was in Herod's court. I'll go in and see what is happening here."

Mary clutched his arm as he turned away. "Be careful," she said, her eyes full of fear. One son was being tried for sedition; if they knew his brother was present, they might try to kill him, too.

James patted her hand. "I will be careful, Mother," he promised.

But before James could leave, Pilate came back out. "I already told you I find no fault in this man. What do you want me to do?" Frustration was evident in his voice. Then, as if he had just realized his out, Pilate remarked, "You have a custom. I should release one prisoner to you for the celebration of the Passover. Here is what I will do. Why don't you let me release unto you the king of the Jews?"

Mary's hope was dashed when a man shouted from the crowd, "Not him. Release to us Bar Abbas."

Mary gasped. "Bar Abbas—the man on the road!" she exclaimed.

Pilate disappeared through the doorway again, and James moved with speed. He had to know what was happening to Jesus. He reached the hall in time to see a soldier add a "crown" to Jesus' outfit. Woven from the thorns that grew along the wall, it sat on top of Jesus' head, the two-inch long spikes pushing into his scalp.

Standing in Judgment

"Scourge him," Pilate said. "Perhaps that will placate these rabid Jews."

Taking Jesus from the palace, the soldiers took him to the Praetorium; the open amphitheater allowed the crowd to watch. Mary moved close to the front, John beside her. James joined them.

"Hail, King of the Jews," one of the soldiers mocked, slapping Jesus' face. The others followed suit, spitting on him as well. The thorns were pushed into his skin, and blood began to flow down his face and neck, staining the top of the purple robe he still wore. A few of the soldiers knelt on the pavement in mock salute. Others added an attitude of pretended prayer.

James looked at his mother. Her face was white, and she held her fist to her heart as if she, too, received every blow that descended on Jesus. James wondered how much more Jesus would take, but the beating went on and on. When it was obvious Jesus could stand no more, Pilate called a halt.

"Behold the man!" Pilate said, his words dropping like stones into the deafening quiet of the crowd. Mary's heart leapt. Perhaps they had had enough.

From the back came a voice: "Crucify him! Crucify him!"

The mob took up the shout, "Crucify him! Crucify him!"[3]

Had it not been for John holding her upright, Mary was sure she would faint. She knew James had moved closer to see what was happening, but her eyes were on Jesus. Blood still dripped and ran from the various cuts on his head. "Where is the compassion these leaders of Israel should have? How can they let one of their own be treated like this?" She didn't realize she had voiced the question aloud until she heard John's voice.

"He isn't one of their own," he said. "He is the Son of God. Listen, Mary. It's something I wrote about Jesus:

> "In the beginning was the Word,
> And the Word was with God,
> And the Word was God.
> The same was in the beginning with God.
> All things were made by him;
> And without him was not anything made that was made.
> In him was life;
> And the life was the light of men;
> And the light shineth in darkness;
> And the darkness comprehended it not."[4]

---

3   See Luke 23:5–11

4   John 1:1–5

Mary's Story

"Where they reject light, darkness comes in," Mary replied. "They have certainly rejected Jesus."

"Remember. He told us he is the light of the world," John replied. "I am beginning to understand some things better."

"I wish I did," Mary replied, her eyes burning as she fastened them on her firstborn son.

"We have a law," one of the scribes spoke up, "and by our law he ought to die, because he made himself the Son of God."

Remembering Jesus' earlier words, fear shook through Pilate's frame. He motioned for the soldiers to return Jesus to the judgment hall. They followed. Again Mary and John waited outside while James went in. Pilate arranged himself on the judgment seat. He had barely settled when a messenger handed him a folded note. Pilate read it, his face turning ashen. Then he glanced keenly at Jesus. He glanced again at the parchment he held in his hand. "My wife writes that I should have nothing to do with you," he said. "She says you are a just man and that she has suffered in a dream because of you."[5]

He looked at Jesus pensively. His face registered his thoughts, from disgust (James could only think it was because of the way the priests acted) to true fear. "Where do you come from?" he asked. The quaver in his voice belied his strength and his reputation as a great soldier.

Jesus said not one word.

"Answer me," Pilate's voice bordered on the hysterical. "Don't you know I have the power to crucify you as they ask, and I have the power to release you?"

"You couldn't have any power at all against me, except if you get it from above. The one who brought me to you has the greater sin," Jesus answered. Pilate thought a moment, then took Jesus out to the steps and addressed the crowd. "Let me release him to you for the Passover," he pleaded.

Again came the rejection and the call for the release of Bar Abbas. "If you let this man go, you are not Caesar's friend. Whoever makes himself a king speaks against Caesar," one of the priests replied.

Pilate took Jesus to the Pavement, the place the Jews called Gabbatha. On the way he thought. If he released Jesus without the Jews' consent, they wouldn't hesitate to say that he was conspiring against Caesar. He had already sent Jesus to Herod with no appreciable results. He must somehow get the Jews to respond to his plea to let Jesus go. One last attempt must somehow be made.

They reached the pavement before he reached a decision. He looked at the Jewish leaders. He could think of only one thing to say. "Behold your king," he announced.

---

5   See Matt. 27:19

Standing in Judgment

"We have no king but Caesar," they shouted.[6]

"What then shall I do with Jesus, who is called the Christ?" Anguish tore Pilate's voice.

Again the hate-filled words thundered through the crowd, "Crucify him!"

"Why? What has he done?" Pilate made one last plea. "I have no reason to sentence him to death."

But the mob was in full voice. Deafening chants of "Crucify him! Crucify him!" filled the air. In despair and disgust Pilate listened. There was no chance he would get this rabble to change their minds. They were determined to crucify a man who deserved, as far as Pilate could see, more than anyone, the kingship of the Jews. He had seen countless so-called messiahs come and go through his courtroom on trial for stealing, kidnapping, even murder, but these people who wanted this man dead had no good reason. They said he claimed to be the king, but he did not claim to be king of anything in this world, and he called himself the Son of God. Pilate couldn't understand it.

He felt there was nothing he could do, however. If he let the man go, a riot would ensue. He would have no choice but to kill a whole crowd of Jews. What difference would it make if one died or a thousand? He called for a basin of water. When it arrived, he summoned one of the soldiers. Bidding him to hold the basin, Pilate stood in front of the mob and held up his hands.

"I am innocent of the blood of this just person. You see to it," he ordered. Then, ceremoniously, so they would all understand, he washed his hands.

"His blood will be on us," a voice called from the crowd, adding "and on our children." The senseless, cruel mob took it up in a chant.

Uncaring hands stripped the bloody robe from Jesus' body, leaving him naked before the jeering crowd. Roughly they replaced his own clothes. Two brawny soldiers carried a heavy cross near and laid it on Jesus' shoulders. He staggered under the load, but began to move.

Mary thought her heart would break. Her beloved son had come to this. He really would be crucified. There was nothing she could do. There was nothing anyone could do but God, and he refused to do it. She didn't understand why. She didn't understand why Jesus hadn't done anything for himself. The man who had walked away from the crowd in Nazareth was allowing them to publicly humiliate him and hang him. Would he really allow them to hang him on a cross? Surely God, or Jesus himself, would still do something. But what was the purpose of this execution, of turning his subjects against himself?

The soldiers moved with Jesus into the crowd and up the road that led to Golgotha, or the Place of the Skull. The mob quieted and parted to let them through. *Now that they are getting their way, they are quiet*, Mary thought bitterly.

At the edge of the crowd, a man stepped forward. "Jesus," he said.

"Is he your friend?" one of the soldiers jeered. "You carry his cross." Roughly they took

---

6 John 9:6–15

Mary's Story

the cross from Jesus' back and placed it on Simon's back. Mary gasped. She didn't know Simon was even there. But he was, and so was Jude; and she saw Cleophas' wife, Mary, and Mary Magdalene. In this hour she should have expected to see Mary Magdalene. There were others, too. The rest of the disciples were there, except she didn't see Judas Iscariot. It comforted Mary to see so many of Jesus' friends in the crowd. Surely someone would do something before Jesus was actually crucified.

The sun shone hot on Mary's head, and she raised her hand to shield herself from its rays. She should have remembered her head covering, but it had been so early and so cool when they left the house. Her mind had been on Jesus. "They have spent all morning destroying Jesus," John remarked, noticing her gesture. "It must be the fifth hour already."

As they passed the prison, two more men joined Jesus, carrying their own crosses. They were going to crucify Jesus, her son, with the common criminals, Mary observed. The crowd stopped for a moment to watch the prisoners join the group, and as they did, a third man came out of the prison doors. Clasping his hands together, Bar Abbas raised them in a sign of victory to the crowd. "I am the Messiah," he proclaimed. Mary felt sick. To think that scruffy convict could think of comparing himself to her perfect son made her physically ill.

If Bar Abbas had expected a reaction from the crowd who had screamed for his release, he was keenly disappointed. Their sole goal was to crucify Jesus; they cared not a whit about the man whom Pilate had released at their request.

Chapter 29

Golgotha

They continued to move slowly down the road. Mary thought her heart would break at every step. Outside the city wall they began climbing Golgotha. She had passed the Place of the Skull every time she came to Jerusalem. She had never thought she would have a reason to go to the dumping grounds of the city, where they hung criminals on crosses.

At the top of the hill, the soldiers told Simon and the other prisoners to drop the crosses. As soon as the crosses were on the ground, the men were laid on them and ropes were brought to lash them to the wood. But it was not enough to satisfy Ananias. Jesus had walked all the way up the hill. Now they removed his clothes. Not even a loin cloth remained between him and the elements. They pushed his bruised back against the rough wood, the crown of thorns still on his head, pushing deeper into his skull as they laid him down.

But as the soldiers began to tie ropes around Jesus, one of Ananias' henchmen stepped forward with a hammer and spikes. Such a crucifixion was reserved for the very worst of criminals. The soldier looked startled, but at a nod from Ananias standing nearby, he shrugged, dropped the ropes, and pounded the nails through Jesus' hands and feet. *Jesus' enemies are determined to see him crucified in the worst way,* Mary realized. *Why do they want to kill the one man who offers them freedom from Roman rule?*

Each blow bruised Mary as she watched. Tears fell unchecked, and again she remembered the prophet Simeon's words from long ago, "A sword shall pierce your own heart also." *Had he known how many thrusts the sword would make?* She heard a woman scream, and then realized, when John held her tightly, it was herself.

It took very little time for the efficient soldiers to fasten men to the crosses. The holes had already been dug. Lifting the crosses into position, they dropped them into the holes with a thud. The nails tore the flesh of Jesus' hands, and blood spurted from the wounds. His bleeding head jerked forward. With an effort he raised it. His voice was surprisingly strong. "I thirst," he said. A soldier soaked a sponge in a container of vinegar, put it on a hyssop branch, and offered it to Jesus to drink. But when Jesus tasted it, he refused to have any more of it.

One of the soldiers had nailed a placard to the cross above Jesus' head. In three languages it proclaimed to the world that Jesus was the King of the Jews. The priests asked Pilate to change

Mary's Story

the words from "King of the Jews" to "He said he is 'the King of the Jews,'" but the potentate, with a sigh of defeat answered, "What I have written, I have written," and turned away in disgust.

Now at the cross, with Jesus hanging there (like the snake on the pole in the wilderness, Mary realized), the priests, the rulers, the scribes, and the Pharisees joined together to taunt him. "If you are truly the Son of God, come down from the cross and save yourself."

"You who said 'destroy this temple and I will build it in three days,' save yourself and come down from the cross!"

"He saved others; himself he cannot save."

"Let Christ, the king of Israel, descend now from the cross that we may see and believe."[1]

He could. Why doesn't he do it? Mary wondered, hoping he would do just that and prove those enemies wrong. The supporters of Jesus stood at the fringes, weeping, while the leaders of the Jews continued to deride him.

"You think he is a king now?" the questioner turned toward those who wept. "Look at him, helpless—some God!" Turning to face the cross once again, they continued, "Look at your followers. Come down from the cross and prove you are the Christ and we will believe you."[2]

The answer to their taunts came quietly from the voice of Jesus, hanging there in pain: "Father, forgive them; for they know not what they do."[3]

Following the priests' example and the soldiers who had already spat on him in derision, the criminal hanging on the cross to Jesus' right also now taunted him yelling, "If what they are saying is true, if you are the Christ, save us and yourself."[4]

"Yes, save them," the soldiers shouted, jeeringly.

"He can't save anyone, least of all himself," the priests replied.

But the man on the cross to Jesus' left, listening to all that had happened, rebuked his accomplice. "You don't know what you are talking about. Don't you fear God at all? We are condemned justly, for we are being punished for our wickedness, but this man has done nothing for which to be condemned."

Finally Mary was hearing words that warmed her heart. If the criminal being crucified with Jesus knew what kind of man Jesus was, surely the religious leaders would see it. Surely they couldn't be completely blind to Jesus' character. Surely they wouldn't let this charade go on until her precious son died.

The thief turned to Jesus and said, "Sir, remember me when you come into your kingdom."

"What kingdom?" spat out a Pharisee. "What kind of kingdom will a dead man inherit?"

But Jesus answered in his calm voice, "I tell you today, you will be with me in Paradise."[5]

---

[1] See Mark 15:29–32
[2] See Matt. 27:40–42 *KN*
[3] Luke 23:34
[4] Luke 23:39
[5] The exchange between the two criminals on the cross and Jesus is found in Luke 23:39–42.

Golgotha

Jesus then looked at his mother in a way that showed he acknowledged that she was with him now as when he had been born. Seeing John holding her, he said, "Behold your mother. Care for her on my behalf." Addressing Mary, he said, "Behold your son. Let him do what I would do were I able to stay with you."[6] Mary took a deep breath and nodded, buoyed by Jesus' care, but it had become abundantly clear that he would do nothing to save himself.

The sentencing, the walk, the hanging, had all taken less than an hour. It was still hot in the noonday sun, and Mary wished for shade and a cool drink, but neither were to be had on that bald hilltop. But then, as if God granted her wish, shade came. She looked for clouds. But there were none. It simply seemed the sun had grown cooler. The air seemed shadowed, somehow. In the space of a few minutes, the mountaintop grew gradually darker until it was impossible to see her hand in front of her face. The soldiers, who had been gambling over Jesus' clothes, stopped for lack of light.

It was dark for three hours. Mary stood, with John's arm around her, wanting to see the sun. If anything, it seemed even darker around the cross, Mary thought. Then, from the midst of the darkness, Jesus' voice came out in a desperate wail: "My God, my God! Why have you forsaken me?"[7]

There was nothing left. If God had forsaken his only begotten Son, there was nothing anyone else could do. It was hopeless. In spite of God's promises, in spite of the grooming and upbringing Joseph and Mary worked for, Jesus was condemned by God. Mary felt as if the ground she walked on had disappeared from her world. For a moment she was angry at God. *Why did He put me through all this, just to have Jesus die the death of a criminal? What is the purpose of all the hard things Joseph and I went through? Where is the promise of Jesus' kingdom? Why had God made me the butt of all the gossip, all the cruelty of the people of Nazareth, just to have my son end up on a cross? Is God really behind all this? Now he has forsaken Jesus. Surely he has forsaken me, too.*

Perhaps the angels weren't from God at all. Perhaps the whole experience is an extravagant hoax of the evil one. How could God let this happen to me, when I have spent my whole life worshipping him?

The darkness seemed to deepen, and from the cross came the answer to Mary's questions. "Father, into thy hands I commend my spirit." In spite of his feelings of rejection, Jesus gave his spirit to the Father. He was still there. Whether she understood or not, God was still in charge.

The taunts of Jesus' enemies were silenced by the eerie darkness. When they moved restlessly as if to begin their snide remarks again, Jesus' voice sounded from the cross again. "It is finished." For someone so near death, his voice sounded so strong. At the end of that proclamation, the ground began to shake.

The eerie darkness was enough to frighten the priests, Mary thought, falling to her knees as the

---

6   See John 19:26, 27
7   See Mark 15:34

world continued to move all around her. Men, who a few hours before had been so confident of themselves now called upon God, reminding Him of their faithfulness to duty, of their support of the poor, of their ability to keep His commandments. They demanded His protection. On the cross the thief had prayed, "Lord, be merciful to me, a sinner." On the ground beside her, John echoed the thief's prayer. "Lord forgive us as we forgive those who have done this injustice to us." Mary marveled at the differences.

It seemed as if the shaking went on forever, when in reality it lasted only a short while. When the earthquake finished, the darkness began to lighten. The atmosphere grew lighter and lighter. Certain that the God of heaven had heard their pious prayers, the priests and rulers rose to their feet. Frightened that they had lost their prisoners in the strange darkness, the soldiers hurried to the crosses, tightening the ropes, checking the prisoners' health. Death by crucifixion meant a slow death on the cross (caused by asphyxiation, dehydration, or sheer pain), or, after having all their limbs broken, being thrown into the garbage heap.

"This one's dead already," one of the soldiers announced. The centurion in charge walked over to the cross. Unsheathing his sword, he thrust it into Jesus' side. Mary gasped at the downright cruelty the soldier exhibited. Blood and water gushed out in two separate streams.

"He died of a broken heart," John murmured.

Mary thought she, too, would die of a broken heart. Simeon's prophecy of so many years before rang again in her mind, "A sword shall pierce your own heart also." All those painful past experiences she had thought were the sword thrusts were mere pinpricks compared to how her heart hurt now. Her Jesus was dead of a broken heart. It had been too much for him. She still didn't understand why God hadn't changed things. *Has God possibly forsaken Jesus because of his willful disobedience to the calling God has sent him to fulfill? That must be it. In spite of what Jesus said about his spirit, he has forsaken God, so God has forsaken him.*

"If he is dead, take him down," the high priest's voice seemed to come from a long distance. "In fact, take them all down. It isn't seemly to have prisoners hanging on the crosses during the holy day of the Passover, and the Sabbath will begin shortly."

In obedience, the soldiers walked to the crosses. Methodically, they broke the legs and arms of the two thieves, carried the thieves over to the pit, and dropped them into the garbage, ignoring their screams of pain. Mary winced as she heard them. A ladder placed against the center cross allowed a soldier to climb up and remove the spikes holding Jesus in place. His body slumped, then dropped to the ground. As the soldiers moved to pick him up and toss him in the pit with the robbers, a man named Joseph stepped forward. Joseph, she learned later, had gone to Pilate and begged for the body of Jesus. He had bought graveclothes and spices to wrap the body in.

"Let me take his body to be buried," he requested. Mary gasped. In dress he proclaimed himself a Pharisee, a counselor from the temple, but John assured her he was a disciple of Jesus.

Golgotha

Another of the Pharisees stepped forward. John said his name was Nicodemus. Mary remembered him to be the man Jesus talked with under the tree when she overheard them. He carried the spices and winding cloth. Now that she thought about it, neither of them had gone along with the others in their condemnation and ridicule of her son.

John, James, and some of the other men moved in to help. Carefully, they picked up the body of Jesus and dressed him in the winding cloth, carefully placing their herbs, as had been the custom for centuries of Jewish deaths. Carrying him carefully between them, they took him to Joseph's personal tomb. There, since it was so near to the Sabbath, they left him.

The women followed; supporting Mary were Joanna, on one side, and Mary Magdalene, on the other. Cleophas' wife, Mary, was close behind. In her hour of trial, those who had not at first accepted Jesus joined with those whose lives had been less than acceptable. Mary, in spite of her grief, noted the irony of it all.

IX

Afterwards

Chapter 30

Passover Sabbath

That Passover Sabbath was one of the strangest Mary had ever known. Simon, taking the sheep to the temple for slaughter, brought them back, reporting that there was so much confusion that no one was slaughtering anything. There were going to be no sacrifices that day. Mass hysteria erupted as those who had gone into the men's court learned that the temple curtain had been ripped from top to bottom by an unseen hand at the same hour Jesus declared on the cross, "It is finished."

The priests and rulers, returning from their foray to the top of Golgotha, were furious. Although the priest in charge of the sacrifice insisted that he had seen no one in the temple and verified that the rip in the curtain had begun at the top, Ananias was adamant that someone had sneaked into the temple and ripped the curtain while the priest wasn't looking. His anger was ferocious. Everyone was avoiding the high priest as much as possible.

In spite of the Sabbath hours, in light of what had happened, the priests went to Pilate early that morning. "Sir," they said, ingratiating themselves as much as possible with the governor. "We remember that this deceiver said, while he was still alive, 'After three days I will rise again.' Will you command that a watch be set, and the sepulcher guarded until the third day? We are afraid that his disciples will come in the night and steal him away in an attempt to pass it off as a resurrection and so deceive the people."

Exhausted by the events of the previous day, still unsure that he had done the right thing, and exasperated by the priests' behavior, Pilate answered off-handedly, "I give you a watch. You make the grave as sure as you can seal it. Don't bother me anymore."

The Sabbath passed slowly. The family tried to focus on the Passover services, tried to make things somewhat normal. The contrived sameness, the pretended normalcy, drove Mary crazy.

She wanted to scream, *Nothing is the same. Why do you insist on keeping things the same? Jesus is dead. My Jesus is in a borrowed tomb. Nothing is the same.*

Late in the afternoon, some of the disciples came by, one or two at a time. They told her stories of Jesus' work, how he had healed people, how he had resurrected people. "Do you suppose he could resurrect himself?" one suggested.

Mary wanted to believe that, but she couldn't. It was one thing to accept the fact that he could raise people back to life, as he had done to Mary Magdalene's brother, Lazarus. She wanted to say, *But he himself was still alive then. Nobody could raise him- or herself back to life; what an absurd kind of miracle to even imagine. Jesus is dead. Can't they see? Don't they know?* The death knell had been dealt to her dreams. *I will never be the mother of the king whose kingdom will last forever. God made those promises, but God's promises are always conditional. If Jesus had done things the right way, he would be alive. He would have become the king on the throne. There would be no more Herod, no more Caesar, no more Pilate, no more Jews killed for rebelling against the ruling authority.*

Mary spent much time that day reviewing the past, considering the way she and Joseph had raised Jesus. *We should never have listened to Zacharias and Elizabeth. Sure, Joseph had a dream, but God never sent us back to Nazareth to live. It was our lack of faith that had sent us there. If we had settled in Bethlehem, as we had planned at first, Jesus would have been able to attend the schools in Jerusalem. He would have learned to find favor with the priests; he would have learned to befriend people who would help him with his quest for kingship.*

Mary wiped her red-rimmed eyes. She didn't believe she would ever stop weeping. God had called her to do a job, and she had failed Him. Her son was to be the king of Israel, whose kingdom would last forever, and now he was dead. There was no kingdom. There never would be a kingdom. God had given her the Messiah, and she had failed. Her failure hurt as much as Jesus' death hurt. She would never smile again.

In spite of the attempts of her family and the disciples to comfort her, Mary refused to be comforted. *The visit of the Wise Men should have been an omen to me,* she thought. *Kings don't visit commoners. Kings visit kings, and God told me that my son would be the king.* But He didn't tell her how to make him the king.

Mary knew that was where they had failed. They should have asked for the angel to lead them as he had done in the past. They had depended on themselves and not on God. She and Joseph had both let God down. Se knew He would never forgive them for that failure. She almost wished she believed as did the Sadducees that there was nothing after life on this earth. She wished she could believe there was no resurrection or judgment.

She vacillated between thankfulness that Joseph didn't know how things had turned out, and blaming Joseph for not keeping closer to God, for dying before Jesus was fully king, for not being the father God meant him to be. *Had Joseph done what God intended the father of a king to do, Jesus would be king, not dead! The angels talked to Joseph, always; never to me after that first visit. Jesus' death is Joseph's fault!*

Anger replaced sorrow. But it didn't help. Joseph wasn't there to vent the anger on, and Jesus was dead. And she was back to the fact that God would never forgive either of them for failing Him.

Her children came, her daughters, her sons, her grandchildren. She loved them; she responded

Passover Sabbath

to them. But nothing they did or said could change the facts. Mary came and Cleophas. Mary Magdalene came and her sister, Martha, and their brother, Lazarus. She hadn't known these people before. She secretly blamed them for not being the kind of people who would further Jesus' kingship. She blamed the disciples, those uncouth fishermen, for being the wrong kind of people. How could they comfort her? She had lost too much because of Jesus' friendship with them.

Others came too. Joanna, whose husband was Herod's chief steward, Nicodemus, Joseph, who had given Jesus his own tomb. Jesus had made some friends in high places, but they had not helped him be king, and she blamed them for not seeing what should have been done.

Why didn't any of them understand who Jesus was supposed to be? Why hadn't they done as much as they could to make him king? And if they felt they had done as much as they could have, why didn't they do more?

Late in the afternoon, she rested. In the evening she fell into a fitful sleep. Early the next morning, Mary Magdalene woke her. A group of women were going to Jesus' tomb to take the ointments the men had forgotten at the cross. Did she want to go?[1]

Did she want to go? Of course she wanted to go! There would be no kingdom that would last forever. This was the last act she could do for her son. She could at least do that. Yes, she wanted to go! It was a new day. The first day of the rest of forever.

It was still dark when they left the house. They got about halfway there, when suddenly another earthquake took place. The women fell to the ground.[2]

"I wonder how many aftershocks there will be," Mary Magdalene said when the earthquake was over.

"I hope there are not a lot of them," Joanna replied. "I don't know anything I hate more than earthquakes in the dark."

As they neared the garden where the sepulcher was, the sun rose in splendor. The group included Mary (the wife of Cleophas), Joanna, Mary Magdalene, and her sister, among others. Mary resented the inclusion of Mary Magdalene. Why did the other women accept her so easily? What had been between her and Jesus? They wandered a bit through the graves looking for the one Jesus had been taken to.

"We should have brought some of the men with us," Cleophas' Mary said. "Who will roll away the stone?"

"I never thought of that," Joanna replied. "We may have to go back and get them."

But when they found the grave Jesus had been taken to, the stone was rolled away. Mary was sure it had been in place when they left Jesus' body there. Pushing ahead of the other women, she was the first to enter the tomb. Her eyes took a moment to adjust to the darkness, and then

---

1 The story of the tomb and what they found is in Luke 24:1–5 and Mark 16:1–10.
2 See Matt. 28:2

Mary's Story

she saw the graveclothes neatly folded on the slab.

"Why do you seek the living among the dead?" a voice spoke.

Mary jumped backward, nearly knocking Joanna to the ground. A man stood near the entrance dressed in clothes that looked somehow luminous. Mary attributed it to a trick of the sunrise.

"He is not here," the man said. "He is risen."

Mary didn't believe it. He was dead. Someone had stolen his body, but the man's words continued. "Don't be afraid. You are looking for Jesus of Nazareth, who was crucified. He is risen; he is not here. Look, this is the place where they laid him."

The women stood in almost total disbelief. Mary didn't know what to think. Could Jesus really be alive? Dared she believe that he was alive? "Remember what he said when you were in Galilee?" the man continued. "He told you he would be delivered into the hands of sinful men, and be crucified, and rise again the third day."

"I remember he said that," Joanna breathed. "I heard him say that."

"He is risen. Go tell his disciples to meet him in Galilee on the mountain. He is going there before you."

Joy replaced the despair in Mary's heart, but she could hardly believe that her beloved Jesus could really be alive. "Did you hear what the man said?" Mary turned to Joanna. "Is Jesus really alive?"

"He really is alive!" Joanna answered, her voice exultant. "He told us in Galilee that he would not stay dead, that he would rise on the third day. We didn't understand then. He is alive. Let's go tell the disciples. Where is Mary Magdalene?"

Mary didn't care where the Magdalene was. She didn't really care for the woman at all. What she cared about was her son, and if he was alive, she wanted to know where he was.

"Let's go tell the disciples," Joanna repeated.

The disciples. Yes, her sons James and Jude were among Jesus' disciples. They should tell Jesus' brothers and sisters and the rest of the family. Jesus was alive. The women began to run. Instead of tears and sorrow, laughter rang through the morning. Jesus was alive!

Chapter 31

The Empty Tomb

They found some of the disciples gathered at Mary's cousin's house where Mary had been staying for the last two weeks.

"Jesus is alive!" Joanna announced.

"You don't know what you're talking about," James answered flatly.

"There were angels at the tomb. I saw two of them," Mary, wife of Cleophas, answered.

"They told us Jesus is alive."

"I saw only one," Mary objected. "And I thought he was just a man."

"The angel said we are supposed to meet Jesus on the mountain in Galilee where he anointed us," Joanna said.

"Jesus is *not* dead," Joanna said again, but she couldn't convince the men.

At that moment Peter and John came to the door. "Where have they taken Jesus' body?" Peter asked. "Do any of you know?"

"Do you mean his body is not there?" James asked skeptically.

"We should have put a guard over it," Alexander stated flatly.

"Where do you suppose the Pharisees would have taken it to, and why?" asked Rufus meaningfully.

"But the man told us he was risen," Mary objected, sorrow crashing down on her again.

Peter put his arms around her. "Believe me, I would like nothing better than for Jesus to be alive, but someone is playing a large hoax on us. Jesus is not alive. He us dead and someone has moved his body."

"We need to do something about it," John said. "We need to find out what happened." He joined Peter, his arm comfortingly around Mary.

"Don't worry! We will find out what happened!" Alexander declared.[1]

"How did you know about it?" Joanna asked. "We just now returned from the grave."

"Mary Magdalene told us the stone had been rolled away. We went to see, and the body is gone. I was the first one there. I've always been able to outrun Peter," John said not without some pride.

---

[1] "And their words seemed to them as idle tales, and they believed them not" (Luke 24:11).

Mary's Story

"We both looked inside, and we saw the grave clothes lying there, but we didn't see anyone else," Peter added.

"What did the men you saw look like?"

"Young," Mary answered.

"Where's Mary Magdalene now?" Joanna questioned.

"We left her in the garden. She wanted to stay there and weep."

But Mary Magdalene wasn't in the garden. She was at the door, her face radiant. "I've seen him and talked to him," she nearly shouted. "He was in the garden. He came up behind me and asked me why I was crying, and I said, 'because they have taken my Lord and I don't know where they have laid him.' I turned around then and saw this man. I thought he must be the gardener. I said, 'If you have taken him away, tell me where you have laid him, and I will take him away.' I meant to remove his body to a safer place. Maybe Galilee."

Jesus' mother, Mary, bridled. *Mary Magdalene has no right to Jesus' body. Mary Magdalene has no right to Jesus at all!*

"But then he said my name," Mary Magdalene continued. "I knew it was he," she said gleefully. "I called him Master and would have hugged him, but he told me not to touch him, because he hadn't yet ascended to God. He told me to come and tell you that he is ascending to his Father, and our Father; to his God, and to our God." Rapture covered her face. "He called God our Father, too."

Listening, Mary recalled Panthera's words. "He is not your son, Mary. He is God's Son." *And now Mary Magdalene said Jesus has called God her Father, too. How can the great God of heaven be the Father to one such as her?*

"I don't know whom you saw, Mary," Peter said kindly. "But I'm sure it wasn't Jesus. You are right; someone has moved the body and someone is playing tricks on us, but you didn't see Jesus."

"Let's close the door and lock it. They might be looking for us," said Rufus.

"Who, the Jews?" asked John.

"Let's not lock the door." Simon's was a voice of reason. "Let's go to an upper room. Sarah, can stay down here and answer the door if anyone comes, and no one will know the difference."

So they went to an upper room, where they sat discussing the possibilities.

"Someone should accost the priests and discover their part in the disappearance of Jesus' body," James suggested.

"But how can we do that without raising suspicion?" Jude asked. They were quiet a while thinking of the possibilities.

"Perhaps Joseph could approach them," Mary suggested. "It was, after all, his grave that was robbed."

"The priests must have paid those men handsomely to lie to you women and tell you Jesus

The Empty Tomb

was alive," Simon said.

Their plans came together slowly. At lunchtime, Sarah brought some food up to them, and they were still going strong.

Late in the afternoon, they were interrupted by Cleophas and Simon, Mary and Joseph's son. They had returned hurriedly from Emmaus. "I thought you planned to stay at home for a few days," Cleophas' Mary said to her husband.

"I did," he replied, "and Simon was going to help with the carpentry that we needed done, but the most extraordinary thing happened!" He took a deep breath and looked to Simon for support. "We met Jesus on the road to Emmaus," he announced.

"We didn't know who he was at first," Jesus' brother agreed. He walked with us most of the way there, and since it was mealtime when we arrived, we invited him to eat with us. He told us the most amazing things about his ministry while we walked. He asked us why we were sad, and we told him all about Jesus' death. He explained many things to us from the Scriptures, but we didn't even know it was him. He has changed so much since his death. He is much more handsome," Simon said without a trace of envy.

"Then it isn't he," Jude said flatly. "Death doesn't change someone so they are unrecognizable. "

James and Joses agreed with their brother. There was no way a brother wouldn't recognize his own brother. Simon had to be mistaken; it had to be an impostor.

But Simon remained adamant. "We asked him to have the blessing for the food," he said, "and when he raised is hands to bless it, we knew it was him. He has scars where the nails pierced his hands and feet."

Scars don't heal that fast," Joses protested

"Jesus heals," Simon, Mary's son, answered.

No one had an answer to that, but most were still sure that Jesus couldn't be alive.

"He didn't even eat with us," Cleophas continued the story. "As soon as we discovered who he was, he vanished."

Hope grew in Mary's breast as she listened to her son and brother-in-law relate their encounter. Had those truly been angels in the garden? Were they telling the truth? Was Jesus actually alive? But when they said Jesus had disappeared, her hope plummeted. *Only a spirit can disappear as they say Jesus has done. Perhaps the spirits are playing on our loss. Everyone knows the spirits are from the devil. We must be careful.*

"We need to be careful," Mary said. "Spirits can be bad. And that acts like a spirit to me."

As if she had conjured up the very spirit, Jesus appeared. "Peace be unto you," he said. Total and complete silence reigned for the space of half a minute, then everyone moved at once, trying to get away from the spirit who stood in the middle of the room. Mary thought fear would choke her and knew the others felt the same way. Simon, Joses, James, and Jude gathered close around

Mary's Story

her. Cleophas, with his arm around his Mary, pulled her into a corner. Joanna and the other women crowded behind the other disciples.

"Why are you scared?" the spirit spoke. "Why do you think I am a spirit? Look at my hands." He held them out to show the obvious scars from the nails. "Look at my feet." Scars from the wounds of the spikes showed plainly on his feet. Come touch me and see it's me. A spirit doesn't have flesh and bones as I have."

Mary was the first to move. She knew his voice. *Can my beloved son be alive?* She could see by the faces around her that they were more happy than afraid, but that Jesus himself was alive and standing among them was almost too much to accept.

"I told you he was alive," Simon exulted.

Mary looked at her son. If he was so sure, perhaps this was Jesus.

"Give me something to eat," he said.

Mary reached behind her to the table. In a dish was a leftover piece of broiled fish and a bit of honeycomb. She picked up the dish and handed it to him. All eyes were upon Jesus as he dipped the fish into the honey and ate it.[2]

"Spirits don't eat food," he remarked, handing the dish back. "Thank you."

He looked around at the faces he loved. "This is what I tried to tell you while I was still with you, before they killed me. Everything must be fulfilled that Moses and the prophets wrote, and the things that are in the Psalms about me."[3]

"You will never reach heaven by your own works, as the Pharisees are trying to do. I have told you before. Only by relying on the mercy of God and the righteousness of Christ can you be saved. This gift is only possible because I came down here from heaven and lived among you and died, and was resurrected. It was important that I suffer, that I die, and that I rise from the dead the third day. Because of that, you can repent, and your sins are forgiven. You must preach this among all nations. Start here in Jerusalem. This is your calling. This is the reason you are my disciples. You are witnesses of these things.

"I will send you the Comforter. Wait here in Jerusalem until you receive his power from on high.[4] Then go to all the world and preach the good news to everyone you meet. He who believes and is baptized shall be saved, but those who don't believe you, will be damned.

"These things will happen to those who believe: In my name they will cast out devils, and they will speak with new tongues; they will take up serpents, and if they drink any deadly thing, it won't hurt them; they shall lay hands on the sick and heal them.[5]

"All power is given to me in heaven and on earth," Jesus continued. "Go, therefore, and teach all nations, baptizing them in the name of the Father, and of the Son, and of the Holy

---

2   See Luke 24:41–43
3   See Luke 24:44
4   See Luke 24:46–49
5   See Mark 16:15–18

The Empty Tomb

Spirit. Teach them to observe all the things I have commanded you; and behold, I will be with you always, even to the end of the world."[6]

Did I hear right? Jesus will never leave us again? He is alive! He will be with us to the end of the world. He had never lied, and Mary knew he was telling the truth now. *In spite of everything that happened, or because of everything that happened, Jesus would now be the king he was born to be.* As if he could read her thoughts, Jesus turned to Mary.

"You believe in God," he said.

She nodded.

"Believe also in me." His seemed to be telling her more than his words were. "My kingdom is not of this world." He repeated what he had said to his disciples on the Mount of Olives the night the soldiers came to take him. Then he left. He left the same way he came. He was there, and then he was gone. Simon looked at Mary, Joses, James, and Jude, "I told you he was alive," he said.

The next day the stories started coming back to them. The earthquake they had felt the morning Jesus rose from the grave was God calling his Son. There were the guards that had been watching the tomb. They fell down like dead men when the angel appeared and called Jesus to arise. The priests had paid them a lot of hush money to not tell the story, but they told it anyway. They said the angel looked like lightning and his clothes were white as snow.

Not only that, but a lot of graves were opened and some who once were dead were now alive, their resurrection having been witnessed by others. Mary looked at her boys. *Could it be true? Were people actually alive? Was Jesus' cousin John alive? Was Joseph?* The story came that John was alive and had appeared to Herod. "I wish I could have seen the look on Herod's face when he saw him," Jude nearly shouted.

And then the day came when they saw Joseph for the first time since he had died. They had gotten used to seeing people they thought were in their graves walking around. But to see Joseph! Mary wrapped her arms around him and didn't want to ever let go.

She told him all that had happened to Jesus and the other boys since his death. "Now Jesus will be the king he was meant to be," she said.

"Oh, Mary. You don't understand. Jesus will never be king on this earth. His kingdom is in heaven. I will go there with him, and John and the others he has raised, but you won't go with us just yet. You must continue to live here on earth and eventually reach the end of your life. It may be years before Jesus comes back. But he will come back to get everyone who loves him. But you won't know how many years have passed since your death. You will be in your grave, and it will seem as if you had just gone to sleep, and Jesus will come. He'll take you to heaven and I'll be there, Mary."[7]

---

6   Matthew 28:18–20
7   See Matt. 27:52, 53

Mary's Story

It was eight days after Jesus had returned from the grave that he finally saw Thomas Didymus. Thomas hadn't been with the group in the upper room when they first saw Jesus. James brought the story home to Mary.

"We have seen the Lord," Peter had told him.

"Unless I see the nail scars in his hands or feet, unless I can touch the scar on his side, I won't believe." was Thomas' reaction.

They were in Peter's house eating a meal when Jesus appeared among them again.

"Peace be unto you," he said.

Peter laughed when Thomas jumped. "See, I told you he was resurrected."

"Here," Jesus said. "You said you wouldn't believe unless you touched my hands and side. Go ahead. Touch me."

Thomas touched his scars with awe on his face. "My Lord and my God!" he exclaimed.

"Thomas, because you have seen me, you believe. Blessed are they who have not seen and yet have believed."[8]

---

[8] See John 20:24–29

Chapter 32

The Last Forty Days

Although Mary still didn't understand Jesus' mission, she began to accept some things. Jesus wasn't her son the way the others were; Panthera had reminded her. He was the Son of God, and she had almost forgotten that he was hers on loan. No, she hadn't even realized that he was hers on loan. He had replaced himself to her with John. She lived with John now. She wasn't sure how she felt about that. For so many years Jesus had been her son. She had loved him as much or more than she had her other children. It was too hard to give him up. Joseph told her she was giving him to the whole world, but she knew she was giving him back to his real Father.

Jesus had said that his mission was to be born, to live, to die, so that she and others might be saved. Jesus' words on the cross came back to echo in her mind. "It is finished." His work was done. When he died on the cross, he fulfilled the purpose for which he had been born. She felt so thankful that God had seen fit to use her and Joseph to be parents to God Himself. Now she felt humbled by that responsibility; so grateful was she that she hadn't realized what was happening until it was all over.

She remembered her thoughts and those dark hours of the Sabbath following Jesus' death. She remembered how she had wished she could believe as the Sadducees. She remembered the loss of hope, the wishing for no judgment. And she began to hope again.

"Though your sins be as scarlet, they shall be white as snow; though they be red like crimson, they shall be as wool."[1] Jesus had quoted the Prophets so often that she knew scriptures by heart herself.

Is that Jesus' meaning? she wondered. *Is he telling me that he died for my sins and that if I believe in him, he will stand in my place in the judgment? Is he promising me no fear? Is he saying God will never judge me but will judge my son instead? No, I have to stop thinking of him as my son ... God will judge me through His Son?* Suddenly, Mary longed for the peace that kind of judgment would bring.

At that moment Mary, the mother of Jesus, became Mary, one of Jesus' disciples. For forty more days, she followed him along with the others as he explained his mission, their mission, the gospel, to them more fully. She began to understand the stories he told. The story of the sheep

---
1 Isa. 1:18

Mary's Story

pen made sense. "No one may enter the kingdom in any way but by me," Jesus reiterated as he talked to them. "I am the way, the truth, and the life; no one comes to the Father but by me."[2]

Jesus pointed out to them the temple service and how every facet of it had pointed to him and his life, death, and resurrection. He talked about the passages in the Scriptures that foretold his life and mission. Although his disciples said that he had told them these things before, they hadn't understood what he had been saying as they did after he died and came back to life.

John told Mary and his family about Jesus being on the shore of Galilee one day. They had fished all night, he and Simon Peter, Thomas Didymus, Nathaniel, the sons of Zebedee, and two other disciples; they had caught nothing. They were tired and cold and had nothing to show for their night's work. A man stood on the shore and asked them if they had caught anything.

They answered that they hadn't caught anything. "And we were plenty discouraged, I can tell you that," John said.

"Throw your net on the other side," the man had ordered.

"Now, we were tired. We hadn't caught anything all night, but we decided to do what he said anyway. Well, we got such a net-full, we couldn't get it into the boat. We had a little boat there. We were only 200 cubits from the shore and were getting ready to call it a night. When that happened, I said to Peter, 'It is the Lord,' and Peter threw his fisher's coat around him; he was naked and threw himself into the sea and swam to shore.

"We came in the little boat and dragged the net-full of fish with us, and when Peter had counted the fish, there were 153. They were big ones, too. And with all those big fish, the net didn't break at all.

"The Lord had a fire on the shore and bread and fish on it, and we had a grand time eating breakfast with him.

"When we were finished eating, Jesus said to Peter, 'do you love me more than these?'

"And Peter answered, 'Yeah Lord, you know I love you.'

"'Feed my lambs,' Jesus said.

"'Do you love me?'

"'Yeah, Lord. You know I love you.'

"'Feed my sheep.'

"The third time Jesus asked the same question, Peter was getting hot under the collar. 'Simon, son of Jonas, do you love me?'

"And he answered, 'Lord, you know all things. You know I love you.'

"'Feed my sheep.'

"So we're to feed his lambs and his sheep. We must go to Jerusalem." They left that day.[3]

It made sense to her now, Mary reflected as they traveled to Jerusalem. She could praise

---

2   The story is found in John 21:1-17.
3   See John 21:15–17

The Last Forty Days

God, understand God, believe God, and believe in the Son God had sent her. She could even accept Mary Magdalene, which was a good thing, since the Magdalenes stayed with them nearly all the time. She learned that Jesus had cast seven devils out of Mary. No wonder Mary loved him so much.

There were about a 120 people at the ascension of Jesus. They had no idea when they first started that it was going to be an ascension, but that's what it turned out to be.

Jesus told them to wait in Jerusalem until they got the promise of the Father. "You will be baptized with the Holy Ghost not many days hence," He told them. "And you will receive power after the Holy Ghost has come upon you; and you shall be my witnesses in Jerusalem, and in all Judea, and in Samaria, and to the uttermost parts of the earth."[4]

Bethany was special to Jesus. Mary wasn't surprised when He led them there. She was surprised when He blessed them.[5] She reflected that Jesus had done many surprising things. And then he went up into heaven. And all those people who were resurrected when he was, went up with him. Mary wanted to go with them right then, but she couldn't. There was work to do here. But he would come again. Maybe before she died.

They were looking up into the clouds where Jesus had disappeared, when two angels appeared by their side. "Why do you stand gazing up into heaven?" the angels said. "This same Jesus that you have seen go into heaven shall so come in like manner as you have seen him go."[6]

How fitting, Mary thought. *There were angels at the beginning of his life on earth. And angels at the end.*

She turned to John. "Well, he said to wait here, so we'll wait."

---

4 See Acts 1:8
5 See Luke 24:50, 51
6 See Acts 1:10, 11

We invite you to view the complete
selection of titles we publish at:

www.TEACHServices.com

Scan with your mobile
device to go directly
to our website.

Please write or email us your praises, reactions, or
thoughts about this or any other book we publish at:

P.O. Box 954
Ringgold, GA 30736

info@TEACHServices.com

TEACH Services, Inc., titles may be purchased in bulk for
educational, business, fund-raising, or sales promotional use.
For information, please e-mail:

BulkSales@TEACHServices.com

Finally, if you are interested in seeing
your own book in print, please contact us at

publishing@TEACHServices.com

We would be happy to review your manuscript for free.

www.ingramcontent.com/pod-product-compliance
Lightning Source LLC
Chambersburg PA
CBHW081917180426
43199CB00036B/2768